A Directory of

PUBLIC GOLF COURSES

in

NEW YORK STATE

By Gail M. Lampman
I. Putnam, Inc.

Chapel Street Publishing
Seneca Falls, NY 13148

This book is available at a special discount when ordered in bulk quantities. For information, contact Golf Special Sales Department, I. Putnam, Inc., P.O. Box 444, Big Flats, NY 14814.

A Directory of Public Golf Courses in New York State

Published by:
Chapel Street Publishing
43 Chapel Street
Seneca Falls, NY 13148-1348

Cover Photo from:
"The Beauty of Golf in New York State"
by John Francis McCarthy
Available at your local pro shop, bookstore, or write:
"Beauty of Golf", P.O. Box 2264, Auburn, NY 13021

Cover design by:
PS Graphic Design
Elmira, NY

Printed in the USA - First Edition

DEDICATION

This book is dedicated to my husband, Earl Lampman, the man who leaves the quest for the "right" course up to me!

ACKNOWLEDGMENTS

While this book was inspired by my personal experience, it would not have been possible without the efforts of my staff at I. Putnam, Inc. I would like to offer my special thanks to Mr. Don Terry, editorial advisor, for countless hours of work and support in making this a reality. Much appreciation goes to Amy Evans, Tamara Abbott, and Geneva Mosher for many days at the phones and computers accumulating and inputting data.

TABLE OF CONTENTS

PREFACE

Golf...a game that can best be described by the most uncommon pairing of terms: frustrating-enjoyable, relaxing-intense, mind clearing-totally absorbing. The ball gets to "lie", but the golfer can't. A "mulligan" is not Irish stew, a "chip" belongs on the green, not on one's shoulder. A game that is played by millions, but mastered by few...that is the wonderfully exasperating game of golf.

My husband and I decided to take up this game several years ago, and choosing to combine our desire to travel and love for golf, we purchased a motor home. We packed our bags, loaded our clubs, and hit the highways, intent on enjoying the challenge of playing a variety of courses in our home state of New York and across the country.

A personal frustration soon developed. I was spending a portion of each sunny day shut up in a phone booth, walking my fingers through the yellow pages, in search of a nearby golf course, with an open tee time and reasonable green fees.

This directory is the result of that frustration. It was my goal to compose a guide that would provide all the necessary information to enable a traveler to quickly select a course to play, in any area of New York State, by simply looking it up in the directory.

New York State, with its rolling terrain, panoramic fairways, and plush greens, offers a wide variety of courses for golfers of all levels. Playing the luxurious courses is always a pleasure, but with two people playing, cost must often be a factor. Many of the less expensive courses listed are well maintained and quite challenging. This directory provides all the information you need to select a golf course suitable to your liking. So grab your clubs, stick this book in your bag, and get out to play a great round of golf.

Gail M. Lampman
President
I. Putnam, Inc.

INTRODUCTION

This directory is the result of a need for current, up-to-date information on more than four hundred beautiful public golf courses in New York State. It includes information such as green fees, par, dress code, amenities, and special packages available for each course that responded to our requests for information.

Our hope is that everyone who enjoys golf as much as we do, will want to visit as many courses as possible, and record their scores and date played. A section is included after each listing, for score validation by the pro or course manager.

Many courses have agreed to extend a one time, ten-percent discount to players who bring this book in with them and request the discount. Every effort has been made to include accurate information on each course. If information is incorrect or incomplete, we welcome any changes and will gladly make the corrections in the next edition.

All listing information was verified with each member firm prior to publication. I Putnam, Inc. cannot and does not, guarantee the correctness of all information furnished them, or the complete absence of errors and omissions, hence, no responsibility for same can be, or is, assumed.

We hope you enjoy this book and the beautiful golf courses waiting to be played in New York State.

How to Use This Directory:

The information in this directory is organized alphabetically by county, city, and golf course. Counties are shown in a black bar which indicates the beginning of the listings in that county. (A map is provided for reference on page X showing the relative location of each county).

COURSE LISTINGS

The name of each course appears in a box under the name of the city or town where that course is located, along with the address and zip code of the course. A few listings are incomplete due to the lack of information available at press time.

HOURS

Most courses are open during daylight hours, but some open earlier, and times are shown opposite "Hours Open".

AVERAGE GREEN FEES

We have tried to provide a range of green fees, but some courses have supplied the actual green fees for the 1993 season, and they are listed. Fees sometimes vary, depending on when you play. All fees are subject to change after publication.

Special rates have been included and some courses have agreed to extend an extra 10% discount to anyone who brings this book in with them and requests the discount. This information is shown at the bottom of each listing.

CREDIT CARDS

If a course accepts credit cards, the acceptable cards are usually listed and the name of the card is given as initials, such as MC for MasterCard or AMEX for American Express.

SEASON

The "Season" listing is the *normal* season when a course is open. Many courses extend their season when weather permits, but some courses close on a set date. We recommend calling first when you plan to play either early in the spring or late in the fall.

AMENITIES

Amenities can be anything extra offered at a course such as lessons, driving range, locker room and sauna, or swimming pool.

DRESS CODE

Most courses have a minimum dress code for golfers and that is shown in the "Dress Code" section. Generally, shirts are required and short shorts are prohibited.

TEE TIMES

If a tee time is required, or recommended, that information is shown. During especially busy times, such as weekends, it is always a good idea to request a tee time first. Phone numbers shown will usually connect you with the club house or pro shop.

PACKAGES AVAILABLE

If there are any packages available with area hotels, restaurants, or other sponsors, a "Yes" will appear near the bottom of the listing...call the course for complete details.

We certainly hope this book proves to be a valuable tool for you to use while you enjoy golfing in New York. Good luck!

PUBLIC GOLF COURSES
in
NEW YORK STATE

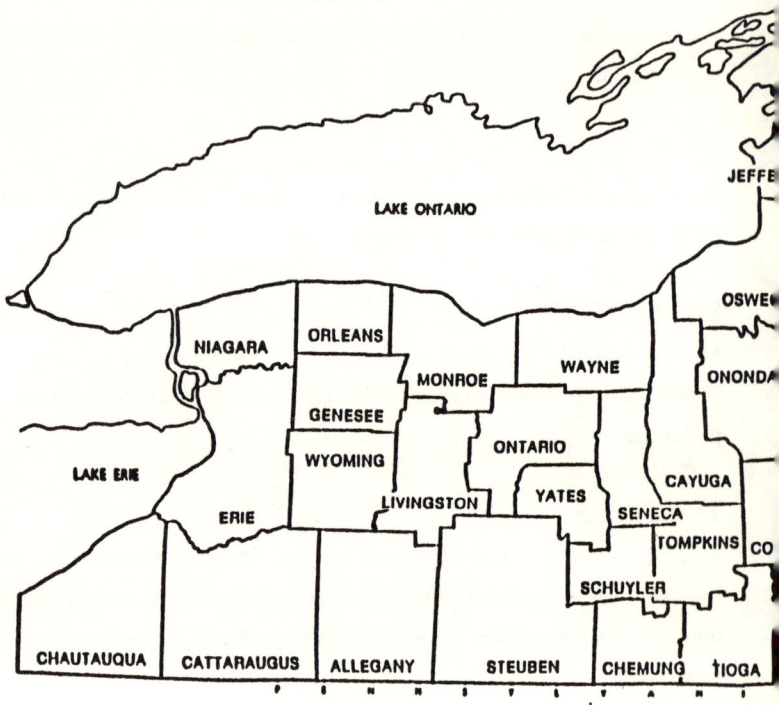

From the rolling hills of the Finger Lakes, to the locust lined fairways of the Catskills; from the fertile Hudson Valley, to the panorama of the Niagara Frontier...golfing in New York State offers hours of pleasure on miles of scenic greenery, challenging all to experience the beauty of this fascinating game in an unforgettable setting.

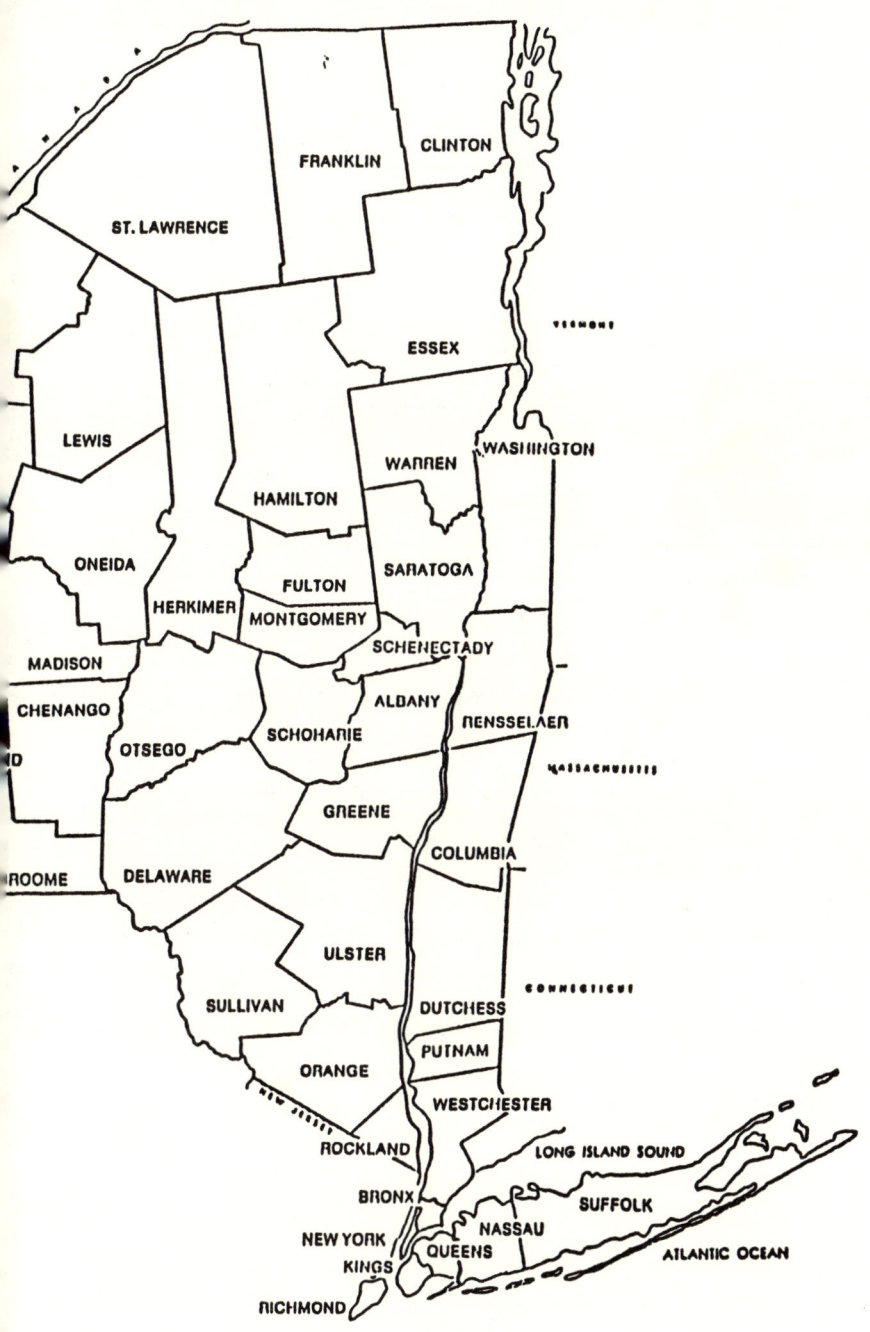

COURSE LISTINGS

Albany

The New Course at Albany
65 O'Neil Rd. • Zip 12208

Phone	(518) 438-2208 (Starter), (518) 489-3526 (Pro shop)
Hours Open	Mon. 9 AM-dusk, Tues.-Fri. 8 AM-dusk, Sat. & Sun. 6:30AM-dusk
Average Green Fees	$10 - $20
Special Rates?	No
Credit Cards	Yes (Pro shop purchases only)
Season	April 1 - November 7
Amenities	Pro shop, lessons, snack bar, liquor bar, driving range, lockers, restaurant, showers, tennis, x-country skiing
Dress Code	No tank tops
Tee Time Required?	Recommended - call starter
Golf Packages Available?	No
10% discount available?	No

Validation _____ Score_____ Date _____

# of Holes	18	Par	72	Carts	YES	Clubs	YES

Guilderland

Hiawatha Trails G.C.
State Farm Road • Zip 12084

Phone	(518) 456-9512
Hours Open	Daylight hours, closed Mondays
Average Greens Fees	$10 and under
Special Rates?	No
Credit Cards	No
Season	April - October
Amenities	Snacks
Dress Code	No
Tee Time Required?	No
Golf Packages Available?	No
10% discount available?	Inquire

Validation _____ Score_____ Date _____

# of Holes	18	Par	54	Carts	PULL	Clubs	$5

Guilderland

Western Turnpike

Rt. 20 Western Ave. • Zip 12084

Phone	(518) 456-9837
Hours Open	7 AM to dark
Average Green Fees	$16 wkdays, $18 wkends
Special Rates?	No
Credit Cards	No
Season	April - October 31
Amenities	Pro shop, lessons, bar, restaurant
Dress Code	No tank tops or cutoffs
Tee Time Required?	Wkends
Golf Packages Available?	No
10% discount available?	No

Validation _____ Score_____ Date _____

# of Holes	9/9/9	Par	36/35/36	Carts	$18	Clubs	YES

Guilderland Center

French's Hollow Fairways

Hurst Rd. • Zip 12085

Phone	(518) 861-8837
Hours Open	Daylight hours
Average Green Fees	$8 - $12 wkdays, $14 wkends
Special Rates?	Senior citizens $6.50 M-W-F
Credit Cards	No
Season	Mid April - mid October
Amenities	Snack bar
Dress Code	Shirts & shoes must be worn at all times
Tee Time Required?	No
Golf Packages Available?	No
10% discount available?	Inquire

Validation _____ Score_____ Date _____

# of Holes	9	Par	37	Carts	$9	Clubs	NO

Latham

Mill Road Acres G.C.

30 Mill Rd. • Zip 12110

Phone	(518) 785-4653
Hours Open	7 AM to 7 PM
Average Green Fees	$7 wkdays., $9 wkends
Special Rates?	Senior citizens
Credit Cards	Yes (restaurant only)
Season	March - November (weather permitting)
Amenities	Pro shop, lessons, bar, restaurant, driving range, golf pro available April - Sept., gift certificates
Dress Code	Proper golf attire
Tee Time Required?	Recommended
Golf Packages Available?	No
10% discount available?	Yes

Validation _____ Score _____ Date _____

# of Holes	EXEC 9	Par	29	Carts	$9/$15	Clubs	$5

Ravena

Sycamore Golf Course

Rt. 143 • Zip 12143

Phone	(518) 756-6635
Hours Open	7 AM to dark
Average Green Fees	$16
Special Rates?	No
Credit Cards	Pro shop only
Season	April - October (weather permitting)
Amenities	Snack bar, dining room, pro shop
Dress Code	No
Tee Time Required?	Yes
Golf Packages Available?	No
10% discount available?	Inquire

Validation _____ Score _____ Date _____

# of Holes	18	Par	72	Carts	$20	Clubs	NO

Six-S Country Club

Transit Bridge • Zip 14711

Phone	(716) 365-2201
Hours Open	Continuous (weather permitting)
Average Green Fees	$10 and under
Special Rates?	wkends and Holidays
Credit Cards	No
Season	March - November
Amenities	Pro shop, bar, restaurant
Dress Code	Proper golf attire
Tee Time Required?	No
Golf Packages Available?	
10% discount available?	Yes

Validation _____ Score_____ Date _____

# of Holes	27	Par	72/36	Carts	$8/$16	Clubs	NO

Evergreen Golf Course

8212 Halls Rd. • Zip 14715

Phone	(716) 928-1266
Hours Open	Daylight hours
Average Green Fees	$8/$10-wkdays, $9/$12-wkends/holidays
Special Rates?	No
Credit Cards	No
Season	April 1 - November 1
Amenities	Pro shop, bar, restaurant
Dress Code	Shirts must be worn at all times
Tee Time Required?	Wkends
Golf Packages Available?	No
10% discount available?	Inquire

Validation _____ Score_____ Date _____

# of Holes	9	Par	36	Carts	$8/$16	Clubs	NO

Mosholu Golf Course

Jerome & Bainbridge Ave. • Zip 10467

Phone	(718) 655-9164
Hours Open	Daylight hours (summer),
	8 AM - 4:30 PM (winter)
Average Green Fees	$10 - $14
Special Rates?	For Senior Citizens
Credit Cards	MC/VISA for reservations only
Season	Late March - December (weather permitting)
Amenities	Driving range, snack bar
Dress Code	No
Tee Time Required?	Wkends
Golf Packages Available?	
10% discount available?	Inquire

Validation _____ Score_____ Date _____

# of Holes	9	Par	35	Carts	$12/$21.50	Clubs	$9.75

Split Rock Golf Course

870 Shore Rd. • Zip 10464

Phone	(718) 885-1258
Hours Open	Daylight hours
Average Green Fees	$14/wkdays,$16/wkends,$8/wkdays,$9/wkends
Special Rates?	For senior Citizens
Credit Cards	VISA/MC
Season	All year (weather permitting)
Amenities	Putting green, chipping green, snack bar, 2 half-way houses
Dress Code	No tank tops or short shorts
Tee Time Required?	Wkends only
Golf Packages Available?	Several
10% discount available?	Yes

Validation _____ Score_____ Date _____

# of Holes	18/18	Par	70	Carts	$21.50/$15.50	Clubs	$25

Bronx

Van Cortlandt Park G.C.

VanCortlandt Park S. • Zip 10471

Phone	(718) 543-4585
Hours Open	Daylight hours
Average Green Fees	$14 wkdays, $16 wkends
Special Rates?	Twilight $8 & $9 wkends
Credit Cards	MC/VISA
Season	April - October (weather permitting)
Amenities	Snack bar
Dress Code	No
Tee Time Required?	Recommended
Golf Packages Available?	Please call for details
10% discount available?	Yes

Validation _____ Score _____ Date _____

# of Holes	18	Par	70	Carts	$21.50	Clubs	$10.00

Belden

Belden Hill Golf Course
1820 NY Rt. 7 • Zip 13787

Phone	(607) 693-3257
Hours Open	Daylight hours
Average Green Fees	$10 and under
Special Rates?	Senior Citizens
Credit Cards	No
Season	May - October
Amenities	Bar, restaurant
Dress Code	No
Tee Time Required?	No
Golf Packages Available?	Group tournaments/Dinner bookings
10% discount available?	Yes

Validation _____ Score _____ Date _____

# of Holes	9	Par	36	Carts	YES	Clubs	YES

Binghamton

Dimmock Hill Golf Course
638 Dimmock Hill Rd. • Zip 13745

Phone	(607) 729-5511
Hours Open	Daylight hours
Average Green Fees	$10 and under
Special Rates?	M - F before 3 PM $5, Senior Citizens $5 - $6
Credit Cards	No
Season	April - November
Amenities	Pro shop, bar, restaurant
Dress Code	No
Tee Time Required?	No
Golf Packages Available?	Yes
10% discount available?	Inquire

Validation _____ Score _____ Date _____

# of Holes	9	Par	34	Carts	YES	Clubs	YES

Binghamton

Ely Park Golf Course

Ridge Rd. • Zip 13905

Phone	(607) 772-7231
Hours Open	Daylight hours
Average Green Fees	$10 wkdays, $11 wkends
Special Rates?	$7.50/9 holes, Seniors $9 -$10
Credit Cards	No
Season	Mid April - October
Amenities	Pro shop, lessons, bar, restaurant
Dress Code	Shirts and shoes required
Tee Time Required?	Wkends & holidays
Golf Packages Available?	Call for details
10% discount available?	Inquire

Validation _____ Score_____ Date _____

# of Holes	18	Par	71	Carts	$1/hole	Clubs	NO

Chenango Bridge

Four Seasons

Rt. 12A, Kattelrielle Rd. • Zip 13745

Phone	(607) 648-3300
Hours Open	Daylight hours
Average Green Fees	$6.50/$11
Special Rates?	Senior Citizens and juniors
Credit Cards	No
Season	St. Patrick's Day - weather permitting
Amenities	Pro shop, restaurant, snack bar
Dress Code	No
Tee Time Required?	No
Golf Packages Available?	Call for details
10% discount available?	No

Validation _____ Score_____ Date _____

# of Holes	9	Par	30	Carts	$6.50	Clubs	$5

Chenango Valley State Park

153 State Park Rd. •Zip 13746

Phone	(607) 645-5251
Hours Open	Daylight hours
Average Green Fees	$7/$12 wkdays, $8/$14 wkends
Special Rates?	Senior Citizens & juniors $4/$6
Credit Cards	Pro shop only
Season	Mid April - Mid November
Amenities	Clubhouse, pro shop
Dress Code	
Tee Time Required?	Wkends & Holidays, 6 AM - Noon
Golf Packages Available?	
10% discount available?	Inquire

Validation _____ Score _____ Date _____

# of Holes	18	Par	72	Carts	$18	Clubs	

Conklin Players Club

Conklin Rd. • Zip 13748

Phone	(607) 775-3042
Hours Open	
Average Green Fees	$10 - $11/9 holes, $17 - $20/18 holes
Special Rates?	
Credit Cards	
Season	
Amenities	
Dress Code	
Tee Time Required?	
Golf Packages Available?	
10% discount available?	Inquire

Validation _____ Score _____ Date _____

# of Holes	18	Par	72	Carts		Clubs	

Deposit

Scott's Oquaga G.C.
Oquaga Lake Rd. • Zip 13754

Phone	(607) 467-3094
Hours Open	8 AM - 6 PM
Average Green Fees	$9 wkdays, $10.50 wkends & holidays
Special Rates?	After 4 PM
Credit Cards	No
Season	May 31 - October 1
Amenities	Restaurant nearby
Dress Code	No
Tee Time Required?	No
Golf Packages Available?	Call for details
10% discount available?	Yes

Validation _____ Score_____ Date _____

# of Holes	9/9	Par	32/36	Carts	$9/$16	Clubs	YES

Endicott

En-Joie Golf Course
722 W. Main St. • Zip 13760

Phone	(607) 785-1661
Hours Open	Daylight hours
Average Green Fees	$18 - $20
Special Rates?	$12 for Senior Citizens, $9 for juniors
Credit Cards	No
Season	May - weather permitting
Amenities	Pro shop, lessons, bar, restaurant, home of the PGA Tours' BC Open
Dress Code	No
Tee Time Required?	Call
Golf Packages Available?	No
10% discount available?	Inquire

Validation _____ Score_____ Date _____

# of Holes	18	Par	72	Carts	$18	Clubs	$10

Endwell Greens Golf Club
3675 Sally Piper Rd. • Zip 13760

Phone	(607) 785-GOLF
Hours Open	Daylight hours
Average Green Fees	$16 - $18
Special Rates?	Senior Citizens $11
Credit Cards	MC/VISA
Season	April 1 - December 1
Amenities	Pro shop, lessons, bar, restaurant, banquet rooms, locker rooms
Dress Code	Shirts must be worn at all times
Tee Time Required?	Yes
Golf Packages Available?	Groups
10% discount available?	Inquire

Validation _____ Score_____ Date _____

# of Holes	18	Par	72	Carts	$10/$20	Clubs	$7.50/$15

Ford Hill Country Club
Rt. 26 • Zip 13862

Phone	(607) 692-8938
Hours Open	Daylight hours
Average Green Fees	$10 - $12/18; $7.50 - $8.50/9
Special Rates?	Senior citizens on wkdays
Credit Cards	No
Season	April 1 - November 1
Amenities	Pro shop, bar, restaurant - open til 10PM
Dress Code	Shirts must be worn at all times
Tee Time Required?	Wkend mornings
Golf Packages Available?	No
10% discount available?	No

Validation _____ Score_____ Date _____

# of Holes	9/9/9/9	Par	35/35/35/35	Carts	YES	Clubs	YES

Windsor

Golden Oak Golf Course
Rt. 79 South • Zip 13865

Phone	(607) 655-3217
Hours Open	Daylight hours
Average Green Fees	$9 - $12
Special Rates?	Seniors $6.50 - $7.50 wkdays
Credit Cards	VISA/MC
Season	March 15 - November 15
Amenities	Pro shop, lessons, bar, restaurant
Dress Code	No tank tops allowed
Tee Time Required?	24 hours in advance
Golf Packages Available?	
10% discount available?	Yes

Validation _____ Score_____ Date _____

# of Holes	18	Par	69	Carts	$9	Clubs	$8

Allegany

Birch Run Country Club

Birch Run Rd. Off Rt. 417 • Zip 14706

Phone	(716) 373-3113
Hours Open	Daylight hours
Average Green Fees	$8 - $11 wkdays, $10 - $13 wkends
Special Rates?	No
Credit Cards	No
Season	April 1 - October 31
Amenities	Pro shop, lessons, bar, restaurant, driving range
Dress Code	Yes
Tee Time Required?	No
Golf Packages Available?	No
10% discount available?	Inquire

Validation _____ Score _____ Date _____

# of Holes	9	Par	35	Carts	$7/$13	Clubs	$5

Ellicottville

Holiday Valley Resort Area

PO Box 370 • Zip 14731

Phone	(716) 699-2346
Hours Open	6:30 AM - Dark
Average Green Fees	$22
Special Rates?	After 4 PM
Credit Cards	All major
Season	April 15 - October 15
Amenities	Pro shop, lessons, bar, restaurant
Dress Code	No cutoffs or tank tops
Tee Time Required?	Yes (may call 3 days in advance)
Golf Packages Available?	Yes
10% discount available?	Wkdays only

Validation _____ Score _____ Date _____

# of Holes	18	Par	72	Carts	$20	Clubs	$12

Franklinville

Ischua Valley County Club

Rt. 16 PO Box 147 • Zip 14737

Phone	(716) 676-3630
Hours Open	Daylight hours
Average Green Fees	$9 - $11
Special Rates?	Senior citizens on Thursdays
Credit Cards	MC/VISA
Season	April - October
Amenities	Restaurant, bowling alley, golf shop
Dress Code	Yes
Tee Time Required?	No
Golf Packages Available?	Please call for details
10% discount available?	Inquire

Validation _____ Score _____ Date _____

# of Holes	9	Par	36	Carts	$5	Clubs	YES

Olean

Castle Inn Golf Course

3220 W. State Rd. • Zip 14760

Phone	(716) 372-1050 or (800) 422-7853
Hours Open	10 AM - dark
Average Green Fees	$5 - $10
Special Rates?	Please call for details
Credit Cards	All major
Season	Memorial Day - Labor Day
Amenities	Coffee shop
Dress Code	No
Tee Time Required?	No
Golf Packages Available?	Wkend getaways
10% discount available?	Inquire

Validation _____ Score _____ Date _____

# of Holes	9	Par	3	Carts	NO	Clubs	$1.50

Randolph

Cardinal Hills Golf Course
Rt. 241 Donewango Rd. • Zip 14772

Phone	(716) 358-5409
Hours Open	Dawn - 10 PM
Average Green Fees	$10/9 $16/18 wkdays; $10/9&$18/18 wkends/Hol
Special Rates?	Please call for details
Credit Cards	MC/VISA
Season	March - October
Amenities	Pro shop, snack bar
Dress Code	No
Tee Time Required?	Recommended for wkends & holidays
Golf Packages Available?	Yes
10% discount available?	Inquire

Validation _____ Score _____ Date _____

# of Holes	18	Par	72	Carts	$8/$15	Clubs	Under $5

Salamanca

Elkdale Country Club
Stone Chimney Rd. Rt. 353 • Zip 14779

Phone	(716) 945-5553
Hours Open	Daylight hours
Average Green Fees	$17 wkdays, $22 wkends & holidays
Special Rates?	No
Credit Cards	MC/VISA
Season	April 1 - November 1
Amenities	Pro shop, lessons, bar, restaurant
Dress Code	Proper golf attire
Tee Time Required?	Yes
Golf Packages Available?	No
10% discount available?	Yes

Validation _____ Score _____ Date _____

# of Holes	18	Par	70	Carts	$16	Clubs	NO

St. Bonaventure

St. Bonaventure Golf Club

Rt. 417 • Zip 14778

Phone	(716) 372-7692
Hours Open	7:30 AM - 8 PM
Average Green Fees	$8 wkdays, $10 wkends
Special Rates?	Please call for details
Credit Cards	No
Season	
Amenities	Bar, restaurant
Dress Code	Shirts must be worn at all times
Tee Time Required?	No
Golf Packages Available?	Upon request
10% discount available?	No

Validation _____ Score_____ Date _____

# of Holes	9	Par	36	Carts	YES	Clubs	Under $5

Auburn

Auburn Country Club
E. Lake Rd. Rt. 38A • Zip 13021

Phone	(315) 253-3152(Golf), (315)253-0359(Rest)
Hours Open	7:30 AM - 8:30 PM
Average Green Fees	$14
Special Rates?	Yes
Credit Cards	No
Season	April 1 - October
Amenities	
Dress Code	Yes
Tee Time Required?	Recommended
Golf Packages Available?	Yes
10% discount available?	Yes

Validation _____ Score _____ Date _____

# of Holes	18	Par	70	Carts	NO	Clubs	YES

Auburn

Cranebrook Golf Club
Canoga Rd. • Zip 13021

Phone	(315) 252-7887
Hours Open	8 AM - dusk
Average Green Fees	$6 - $8.50
Special Rates?	Senior citizens
Credit Cards	No
Season	April - October (weather permitting)
Amenities	Snack bar, beer
Dress Code	Shirts required
Tee Time Required?	No
Golf Packages Available?	No
10% discount available?	No

Validation _____ Score _____ Date _____

# of Holes	9	Par	31	Carts	$8 - $12	Clubs	$2.50

Cato

Cato Golf Club

Rt. 34 • Zip 13033

Phone	(315) 626-2291
Hours Open	7 AM - dark
Average Green Fees	$10
Special Rates?	Senior citizens (M-W-F)
Credit Cards	No
Season	April 1 - October 31
Amenities	Pro shop, bar, restaurant
Dress Code	Proper golf attire preferred
Tee Time Required?	First come, first served
Golf Packages Available?	No
10% discount available?	No

Validation _____ Score_____ Date _____

# of Holes	9	Par	35	Carts	YES	Clubs	YES

Cayuga

Indian Head Golf Course

Rts. 5 & 20 • Zip 13034

Phone	(315) 253-6812
Hours Open	Daylight hours
Average Green Fees	$6.50
Special Rates?	For large groups
Credit Cards	No
Season	April 1 - October 31
Amenities	Snack bar, pro shop, driving range, putting green
Dress Code	No
Tee Time Required?	No
Golf Packages Available?	No
10% discount available?	Yes

Validation _____ Score_____ Date _____

# of Holes	9	Par	36	Carts	$8.50	Clubs	$3

Locke

Fillmore Golf Course

Tollgate Hill Rd. • Zip 13092

Phone	(315) 497-3145
Hours Open	7 AM - dark
Average Green Fees	$7 - $12
Special Rates?	Please call for details
Credit Cards	No
Season	Mid April - Mid October
Amenities	Pro shop, lounge, restaurant, banquet facilities
Dress Code	No
Tee Time Required?	Recommended
Golf Packages Available?	Please call for details
10% discount available?	Yes

Validation _____ Score _____ Date _____

# of Holes	18	Par	71	Carts	YES	Clubs	$5

Owasco

Dutch Hollow Country Club

Benson Rd. • Zip 13130

Phone	(315) 784-5052
Hours Open	7 AM - dusk
Average Green Fees	$10 - $20 wkends
Special Rates?	Wkdays
Credit Cards	MC
Season	April 1 - November 15
Amenities	Restaurant, pro shop, driving range
Dress Code	No tank tops
Tee Time Required?	Yes
Golf Packages Available?	Yes
10% discount available?	Yes

Validation _____ Score _____ Date _____

# of Holes	18	Par	71	Carts	$19	Clubs	$12

Meadowbrook Golf Course

Ball Rd. • Zip 13166

Phone	(315) 834-9358
Hours Open	Daylight hours
Average Green Fees	$6.50-$8.50 wkdays, $8-$10 wkends & holidays
Special Rates?	After 6 PM - $5
Credit Cards	No
Season	
Amenities	Snack bar, clubhouse
Dress Code	Shirts & shoes must be worn at all times
Tee Time Required?	No, tee is closed 4 - 6 PM Mon.-Thurs.
Golf Packages Available?	No
10% discount available?	Seniors before noon on wkdays

Validation _____ Score_____ Date _____

# of Holes	9	Par	35	Carts	$8.50/$17	Clubs	$5

Bemus Point Golf & Tennis   72 Main St. • Zip 14712

Phone	(716) 386-2893
Hours Open	Daylight hours
Average Green Fees	$7 - $10 wkdays, $8 - $12 wkends (1992 rates)
Special Rates?	Senior citizens-10% on wkdays
Credit Cards	MC/VISA
Season	April -October
Amenities	Pro shop, lessons, bar, restaurant
Dress Code	Proper golf attire
Tee Time Required?	No
Golf Packages Available?	No
10% discount available?	No

Validation _____ Score _____ Date _____

# of Holes	9	Par	36	Carts	$8/$15	Clubs	$3

Cassadaga Lakes C. C.   55 Frisbee Rd. • Zip 14718

Phone	(716) 595-3003
Hours Open	Daylight hours
Average Green Fees	$7/9 holes
Special Rates?	Inquire
Credit Cards	Yes
Season	April - October
Amenities	Dining room w/full service bar
Dress Code	
Tee Time Required?	No
Golf Packages Available?	
10% discount available?	Yes

Validation _____ Score _____ Date _____

# of Holes	9	Par	35	Carts	YES	Clubs	YES

Chautauqua

Chautauqua Golf Course

Rt. 394 • Zip 14722

Phone	(716) 357-6211
Hours Open	Daylight hours
Average Green Fees	$12 wkdays, $16 wkends, $20-$25 6/26 - Labor Day
Special Rates?	After 4:30PM-$7 pre & post, $13 in season
Credit Cards	MC/VISA
Season	
Amenities	Pro shop, lessons, snack bar, no liquor
Dress Code	No tank tops or short shorts
Tee Time Required?	Yes
Golf Packages Available?	During pre & post season
10% discount available?	Inquire

Validation _____ Score_____ Date _____

# of Holes	9/9/9	Par	36/36/36	Carts	$20	Clubs	YES

Forestville

Tri-County Country Club

RR 39 Box 337 • Zip 14062

Phone	(716) 965-2053
Hours Open	Daylight hours
Average Green Fees	$18 wkdays, $20 wkends
Special Rates?	No
Credit Cards	MC/VISA
Season	Mid April - October
Amenities	Pro shop, bar, restaurant
Dress Code	No tank tops or short shorts
Tee Time Required?	No
Golf Packages Available?	No
10% discount available?	No

Validation _____ Score_____ Date _____

# of Holes	18	Par	71	Carts	$18	Clubs	NO

Fredonia

Hillview Golf Course
4717 Berry Rd. • Zip 14063

Phone	(716) 679-4571
Hours Open	Daylight hours
Average Green Fees	$11 wkdays, $14 wkends
Special Rates?	After 3 PM $8.50, after 5 PM $6.50
Credit Cards	No
Season	April 1 - October 31
Amenities	Pro shop, bar, snack bar
Dress Code	No
Tee Time Required?	No
Golf Packages Available?	No
10% discount available?	Inquire

Validation _____ Score _____ Date _____

# of Holes	18	Par	70	Carts	$15	Clubs	$5

Jamestown

Forest Heights G.C.
Forest Ave. • Zip 14701

Phone	(716) 487-0533
Hours Open	Daylight hours
Average Green Fees	$4.50
Special Rates?	Senior citizens on wkdays - $3.50
Credit Cards	No
Season	April - October
Amenities	Snack bar, equipment, driving range
Dress Code	No
Tee Time Required?	No
Golf Packages Available?	No (season memberships)
10% discount available?	Inquire

Validation _____ Score _____ Date _____

# of Holes	9	Par	27	Carts		Clubs	$2.50

Jamestown

South Hills Country C.lub

3108 Busti Stillwater Rd. • Zip 14701

Phone	(716) 487-1471
Hours Open	7 AM - dusk
Average Green Fees	$12 wkdays, $15 wkends
Special Rates?	Senior citizens
Credit Cards	No
Season	March 1- Decmeber 31
Amenities	Pro shop, bar, restaurant, practice area
Dress Code	No
Tee Time Required?	Wkends & holidays
Golf Packages Available?	No
10% discount available?	Inquire

Validation _____ Score_____ Date _____

# of Holes	18	Par	72	Carts	$6/$9	Clubs	$5

Lakewood

Maplehurst Country C.lub

1508 Big Tree Rd. • Zip 14750

Phone	(716) 763-1225
Hours Open	Daylight hours
Average Green Fees	$14 - $16
Special Rates?	After 5 PM
Credit Cards	MC/VISA
Season	April - November
Amenities	2 teaching pros, restaurant, bar, pro shop
Dress Code	No cut offs, shirts with sleeves must be worn
Tee Time Required?	Wkends only
Golf Packages Available?	Please call for details
10% discount available?	Yes

Validation _____ Score_____ Date _____

# of Holes	18	Par	70	Carts	YES	Clubs	YES

Lakewood

Sunset Valley G. C.
724 Hunt Rd. • Zip 14750

Phone	(716) 664-7508
Hours Open	7 AM - 9 PM
Average Green Fees	$10 & under
Special Rates?	Senior Citizens, ladies & youth under 18
Credit Cards	No
Season	April - September
Amenities	Pro shop, snack shop
Dress Code	No
Tee Time Required?	No
Golf Packages Available?	No
10% discount available?	Yes

Validation _____ Score_____ Date _____

# of Holes	18	Par	EXEC 3	Carts	PULL	Clubs	$2

Mayville

Chautauqua Point G.C.
Highway 430 East • Zip 14757

Phone	(716) 753-7271
Hours Open	7 AM - 9 PM
Average Green Fees	$7 & $9 wkdays, $10 & $12 wkends
Special Rates?	Senior citizens
Credit Cards	All major
Season	April 15 - snowfall
Amenities	Bar & restaurant
Dress Code	Shirts must be worn at all times
Tee Time Required?	Yes
Golf Packages Available?	Yes
10% discount available?	Inquire

Validation _____ Score_____ Date _____

# of Holes	9	Par	35	Carts	$9/$17	Clubs	$2.50

Mayville

Willow Run G. C.
Magnolia • Zip 14757

Phone	(716) 789-3162
Hours Open	Daylight hours
Average Green Fees	$10 and under
Special Rates?	Senior citizens
Credit Cards	No
Season	April 15 - October 31
Amenities	Snack bar
Dress Code	Shirts
Tee Time Required?	No
Golf Packages Available?	No
10% discount available?	Yes

Validation _____ Score_____ Date _____

# of Holes	9	Par	29	Carts	YES	Clubs	YES

Mayville

Woodcrest Golf Course
RR 2, Wallstreet Rd. • Zip 14757

Phone	(716) 789-4653
Hours Open	Daylight hours
Average Green Fees	$5.50 - $9
Special Rates?	Senior citizens
Credit Cards	No
Season	May 1 - October 31
Amenities	Driving range, expanding course will be fullfledged course in 2 years
Dress Code	No
Tee Time Required?	No
Golf Packages Available?	
10% discount available?	

Validation _____ Score_____ Date _____

# of Holes	9	Par	29	Carts	YES	Clubs	YES

Ripley

Lakeside Golf Course
W. Lake Rd. • Zip 14775

Phone	(716) 736-7637
Hours Open	Sunrise - sunset
Average Green Fees	$7/9holes, $11/18 holes
Special Rates?	Senior Citizens
Credit Cards	No
Season	April 1 - October 31
Amenities	Snack shop, pro shop
Dress Code	Shirts required
Tee Time Required?	No
Golf Packages Available?	No
10% discount available?	Inquire

Validation _____ Score_____ Date _____

# of Holes	EXEC 9	Par	33	Carts	$7.50	Clubs	$4

Silver Creek

Rosebrook Golf Course
130 Beebe Rd. • Zip 14136

Phone	(716) 934-2825
Hours Open	Daylight hours
Average Green Fees	$7 - $10 wkdays, $9 - $13 wkends
Special Rates?	Senior Citizens
Credit Cards	No
Season	April - October
Amenities	Limited pro shop, sandwiches
Dress Code	No
Tee Time Required?	Wkends
Golf Packages Available?	No
10% discount available?	Inquire

Validation _____ Score_____ Date _____

# of Holes	9	Par	34	Carts	$7.50	Clubs	$5

Westfield

Pinehurst Golf Course

E. Main Rd. • Zip 14787

Phone	(716) 326-4424
Hours Open	Daylight hours
Average Green Fees	$8/$11 wkdays, $9/$12 wkends
Special Rates?	No
Credit Cards	No
Season	Mid April - mid October
Amenities	Small pro shop, snacks
Dress Code	Proper golf attire
Tee Time Required?	No
Golf Packages Available?	No
10% discount available?	No

Validation _____ Score _____ Date _____

# of Holes	9	Par	72	Carts	$9/$18	Clubs	No

Big Flats

Willowcreek Golf Course

Rt. 352 • Zip 14814

Phone	(607) 562-8898
Hours Open	6 AM - 11 PM
Average Green Fees	$9 & $15
Special Rates?	Please call for details
Credit Cards	All major
Season	March - December
Amenities	Pro shop, lessons, bar, restaurant, drving range
Dress Code	Proper golf attire
Tee Time Required?	Wkends
Golf Packages Available?	Yes
10% discount available?	Greens fees only

Validation _____ Score _____ Date _____

# of Holes	27	Par	72	Carts	YES	Clubs	YES

Elmira Heights

Mark Twain Golf Course

Rt. 14 • Zip 14903

Phone	(607) 737-5770
Hours Open	6:30 AM - til dark
Average Green Fees	$7 - $12
Special Rates?	Senior citizens $1 off, after 3 PM - $7
Credit Cards	No
Season	1st Wed. April - December 31 (weather permitting)
Amenities	Snack bar, locker rooms, practice chip & putt, practice sand traps. "A DONALD ROSS DESIGNED COURSE," USGA ruled.
Dress Code	No tank tops, shirts required
Tee Time Required?	First come, first served
Golf Packages Available?	Please call for details
10% discount available?	No

Validation _____ Score _____ Date _____

# of Holes	18	Par	72	Carts	$8 - $16	Clubs	$4

Horseheads

Soaring Eagles G.C..
Middle Rd. • Zip 14845

Phone	(607) 739-0551(Club), (607) 739-0034 (Park)
Hours Open	6 AM - dark
Average Green Fees	$12 wkdays, $14 wkends & holidays
Special Rates?	Senior citizen residents of NYS
Credit Cards	Concession stand only
Season	April 8 - first Tuesday in November
Amenities	Pro shop, lessons, bar, restaurant, driving range, practice range, putting green
Dress Code	Shirts must be worn at all times
Tee Time Required?	Wkends & holiday, special events
Golf Packages Available?	No
10% discount available?	No

Validation _____ Score _____ Date _____

# of Holes		Par		Carts		Clubs	
	18		72		$18		$5

Waverly

Tomasso's Chemung G.C.
County Rd. 60 RD#1 • Zip 14892

Phone	(607) 565-2323
Hours Open	Daylight hours
Average Green Fees	$10 - $12
Special Rates?	Senior citizens
Credit Cards	No
Season	Year round
Amenities	Pro shop, bar, restaurant
Dress Code	Shirts must be worn at all times
Tee Time Required?	No
Golf Packages Available?	No
10% discount available?	No

Validation _____ Score _____ Date _____

# of Holes		Par		Carts		Clubs	
	18		69		YES		NO

Afton

Afton Golf Course

Lake Rd. • Zip 13730

Phone	(607) 639-2454
Hours Open	Daylight hours
Average Green Fees	$12 - $15
Special Rates?	$9 - $11/9 holes
Credit Cards	No
Season	Weather permitting
Amenities	Pro shop, lessons, bar, restaurant
Dress Code	
Tee Time Required?	
Golf Packages Available?	
10% discount available?	Inquire

Validation _____ Score _____ Date _____

# of Holes	18	Par	72	Carts	$15-$25	Clubs	YES

Greene

Genegantslet Golf Club

Rt. 12 Box 444 • Zip 13778

Phone	(607) 656-8191
Hours Open	6 AM - dark
Average Green Fees	$8 - $12 wkdays, $9 - $14 wkends & holidays
Special Rates?	No
Credit Cards	MC/VISA
Season	March - December (weather permitting)
Amenities	Pro shop, lessons, bar, restaurant, party room
Dress Code	No
Tee Time Required?	No
Golf Packages Available?	No
10% discount available?	No

Validation _____ Score _____ Date _____

# of Holes	18	Par	70	Carts	$9/$17	Clubs	$5

Sundown Golf & Country Club

Hypath Ln. • Zip 13780

Phone	(607) 895-6888
Hours Open	Daylight hours
Average Green Fees	$8 wkdays, $10 wkends
Special Rates?	Senior citizens M - F $6
Credit Cards	No
Season	April - October 31 (weather permitting)
Amenities	Limited pro shop, snack bar, bar
Dress Code	Shirts required
Tee Time Required?	No
Golf Packages Available?	No
10% discount available?	Yes

Validation _____ Score_____ Date _____

# of Holes	9	Par	34	Carts	$9/$15	Clubs	YES

Way Back of Sundown

Ives Settlement Rd. • Zip 13780

Phone	(607) 895-6888
Hours Open	Dawn - dusk
Average Green Fees	$8 - $10
Special Rates?	Senior Citizens M - F $6
Credit Cards	No
Season	April 1 - October 31
Amenities	Snack bar, bar, limited pro shop
Dress Code	Proper golf attire
Tee Time Required?	No
Golf Packages Available?	No
10% discount available?	Yes

Validation _____ Score_____ Date _____

# of Holes	9	Par	34	Carts	$9/$15	Clubs	YES

New Berlin

Riverbend Golf Club
Route 8 • Zip 13411

Phone	(607) 847-8481
Hours Open	Daylight hours
Average Green Fees	$6 wkdays, $7 wkends
Special Rates?	No
Credit Cards	MC/VISA
Season	April - October
Amenities	Pro shop, bar, & restaurant run seperately
Dress Code	Proper golf attire
Tee Time Required?	Wkends & after 4 PM
Golf Packages Available?	No
10% discount available?	Inquire

Validation _____ Score _____ Date _____

# of Holes	9	Par	35	Carts	$8	Clubs	$2

Norwich

Canasawacta C.C.
Country Club Rd. • Zip 13815

Phone	(607) 336-9214 (Club), (607) 336-2685 Pro shop)
Hours Open	7:30 AM -dark
Average Green Fees	$18 - $22
Special Rates?	$10 - $12/9 holes
Credit Cards	MC/VISA
Season	Weather permitting
Amenities	Pro shop, lessons, bar, restaurant
Dress Code	Casual - no tank tops or short shorts
Tee Time Required?	Yes - 2 days advance
Golf Packages Available?	No
10% discount available?	Yes

Validation _____ Score _____ Date _____

# of Holes	18	Par	70	Carts	$15	Clubs	$5/$10

Oxford

Blue Stone Golf Course
Grant & Scott Sts. • Zip 13830

Phone	(607) 843-8352
Hours Open	7 AM - dark
Average Green Fees	$8.50 wkdays, $10.50 wkends & holidays
Special Rates?	$7 - $8.50/9 holes
Credit Cards	Yes
Season	March - December (weather permitting)
Amenities	Restaurant, lounge, pro shop, lessons, club repair & assembly
Dress Code	No
Tee Time Required?	Appreciated
Golf Packages Available?	Yes
10% discount available?	Yes

Validation _____ Score_____ Date _____

# of Holes	18	Par	70	Carts	YES	Clubs	YES

Sherburne

Mountain Top Golf Club
RR1, Box 126 • Zip 13460

Phone	(607) 674-4005
Hours Open	Daylight hours
Average Green Fees	$6/$18 wkdays, $7/$18 wkends & holidays
Special Rates?	Membership
Credit Cards	No
Season	Mid April - 1st snowfall (weather permitting)
Amenities	Bar, snack bar, limited pro shop, driving range
Dress Code	Shirts & shoes required
Tee Time Required?	Recommended for wkends
Golf Packages Available?	No
10% discount available?	Yes

Validation _____ Score_____ Date _____

# of Holes	9	Par	34	Carts	$8/$13.50	Clubs	$4

Peru

Adirondack Golf & C.C.

Rock Rd. • Zip 12972

Phone	(518) 643-8403
Hours Open	6 AM - dark
Average Green Fees	$24 wkdays, $28 wkends
Special Rates?	Senior citizens
Credit Cards	MC/VISA
Season	March - til snowfalls
Amenities	Pro shop, limited restaurant, bar
Dress Code	No cutoffs or tanktops
Tee Time Required?	Preferred
Golf Packages Available?	Please call for details
10% discount available?	Yes

Validation _____ Score _____ Date _____

# of Holes	18	Par	72	Carts	$22	Clubs	$15

Plattsburgh

Bluff Point Golf & C.C.

Lake Shore Rd. • Zip 12901

Phone	(518) 563-3420
Hours Open	Dawn to dark
Average Green Fees	$24 - $29
Special Rates?	Please call for details
Credit Cards	MC/VISA
Season	April 23 - October 31
Amenities	Pro shop, lessons, restaurant catered by Marriott, driving range
Dress Code	Shirts w/collars, no jeans or tee shirts
Tee Time Required?	Yes
Golf Packages Available?	Please call for details
10% discount available?	No

Validation _____ Score _____ Date _____

# of Holes	18Champ	Par	72	Carts	$22	Clubs	$10

North Country Golf Club

Hayford Rd. • Zip 12979

Phone	(518) 297-2582
Hours Open	6 AM - 11 PM
Average Green Fees	$22
Special Rates?	No
Credit Cards	MC/VISA
Season	April 15 - October 31
Amenities	Pro shop, lessons, bar, restaurant, putting green, driving range, storage facilities
Dress Code	No shorts or tank tops, shirts w/collars & sleeves
Tee Time Required?	June - August, also wkends all season
Golf Packages Available?	No
10% discount available?	Inquire

Validation _____ Score _____ Date _____

# of Holes	18	Par	72	Carts	$22	Clubs	$7

Copake

Undermountain G.C.

Undermountain Rd. off Rt.22 • Zip 12516

Phone	(518) 329-4444
Hours Open	Daylight hours
Average Green Fees	$6.50/$10.25 wkdays, $7.75/$13 wkends & holidays
Special Rates?	Senior citizens wkdays
Credit Cards	No
Season	April 1 - November, weather permitting
Amenities	Limited snack bar, beer, soda, juice bar, pro shop, practice green
Dress Code	
Tee Time Required?	Wkends & Holidays
Golf Packages Available?	No
10% discount available?	Inquire

Validation _____ Score _____ Date _____

# of Holes	EXEC 9	Par	32/65	Carts	PULL	Clubs	$2

Copake Lake

Copake Country Club

Off Lakeview Ave, Golf Course Rd. • Zip 12521

Phone	(518) 325-4338
Hours Open	Daylight hours
Average Green Fees	$8/$13 wkdays, $12/$17 wkends
Special Rates?	Senior Citizens M-Th $6/$9, Tues. all $6/$10
Credit Cards	No
Season	May 1 - November 1
Amenities	Snack shop, 4 tennis courts
Dress Code	Shirts required at all times
Tee Time Required?	No
Golf Packages Available?	No
10% discount available?	Inquire

Validation _____ Score _____ Date _____

# of Holes	18	Par	72	Carts	$10	Clubs	NO

Ghent

Meadowgreens Golf Course

Rt. 9H • Zip 12075

Phone	(518) 828-0663
Hours Open	Daylight hours
Average Green Fees	$10 - $15
Special Rates?	Group rates available
Credit Cards	MC/VISA
Season	Year-round as weather permits
Amenities	Pro shop, bar, restaurant
Dress Code	
Tee Time Required?	No
Golf Packages Available?	
10% discount available?	No

Validation _____ Score_____ Date _____

# of Holes	9	Par	36	Carts	YES	Clubs	YES

Valatie

Winding Brook Golf Course

Rt. 203 • Zip 12184

Phone	(518)758-9117
Hours Open	Daylight hours
Average Green Fees	$10 - $20
Special Rates?	
Credit Cards	No
Season	All year
Amenities	Pro shop, lessons, bar, restaurant
Dress Code	No tank tops, short shorts, coolers
Tee Time Required?	Yes
Golf Packages Available?	Yes
10% discount available?	No

Validation _____ Score_____ Date _____

# of Holes	18	Par	72	Carts	YES	Clubs	YES

Cincinnatus

Knickerbocker C.C.

Telephone Rd. • Zip 13040

Phone	(607) 863-3800
Hours Open	Daylight hours
Average Green Fees	$10 and under for all day
Special Rates?	No
Credit Cards	No
Season	Weather permitting - October 31
Amenities	Pro shop, bar, restaurant
Dress Code	No
Tee Time Required?	No
Golf Packages Available?	No
10% discount available?	No

Validation _____ Score _____ Date _____

# of Holes	9/18	Par	35	Carts	YES	Clubs	$2

Cortland

Elm Tree Golf Course

S. Cortland Rd. Rt.13 • Zip 13045

Phone	(607) 753-1341
Hours Open	Daylight hours
Average Green Fees	$10 - $20
Special Rates?	Wkdays
Credit Cards	MC/VISA
Season	March 15 - October
Amenities	
Dress Code	No
Tee Time Required?	No
Golf Packages Available?	Wkdays $20/person, incl. riding cart, greens, lunch
10% discount available?	

Validation _____ Score _____ Date _____

# of Holes	9/18	Par	70	Carts	$1/hole	Clubs	No

Cortland

Willowbrook Golf Club
3267 State Rt. 215 • Zip 13045

Phone	(607) 756-7382
Hours Open	Daylight hours
Average Green Fees	$7/$10 wkdays, $9/$12 wkends
Special Rates?	Wkdays 2 people w/cart $30
Credit Cards	MC/VISA
Season	April 1 - October 31
Amenities	Pro shop, bar, restaurant
Dress Code	No
Tee Time Required?	No
Golf Packages Available?	No
10% discount available?	No

Validation _____ Score_____ Date _____

# of Holes	9/18	Par	70	Carts	YES	Clubs	YES

Marathon

Maple Hill Golf Club
Conrad Rd. PO Box 521 • Zip 13803

Phone	(607) 849-3285
Hours Open	Daylight hours
Average Green Fees	$10 - $20
Special Rates?	Wkdays
Credit Cards	No
Season	April 1 - October 31
Amenities	Restaurant, bar, pro shop
Dress Code	No
Tee Time Required?	Wkends
Golf Packages Available?	No
10% discount available?	No

Validation _____ Score_____ Date _____

# of Holes	9/18	Par	70	Carts	$18	Clubs	$5

Delhi

College Golf

Back River Road • Zip 13753

Phone	(607) 746-4281
Hours Open	7 AM - dusk
Average Green Fees	$10 - $15
Special Rates?	Under 17, Senior citizens, Delhi Tech, after hrs.
Credit Cards	MC/VISA
Season	April - October
Amenities	Pro shop, lessons, snack bar
Dress Code	Sleeve-type shirt
Tee Time Required?	Wkends & Holidays
Golf Packages Available?	Yes
10% discount available?	Merchandise only

Validation _____ Score_____ Date _____

# of Holes	9	Par	36	Carts	$10/$18	Clubs	$5

Franklin

Ouleout Creek Golf Course

HC 87 Box 37 • Zip 13775

Phone	(607) 829-2100
Hours Open	Daylight hours
Average Green Fees	$8 - $11
Special Rates?	Senior citizens
Credit Cards	MC/VISA
Season	March 15 - December 1 (weather permitting)
Amenities	Restaurant, pro shop, lessons, driving net
Dress Code	Shirts required
Tee Time Required?	No
Golf Packages Available?	No
10% discount available?	Yes

Validation _____ Score_____ Date _____

# of Holes	9	Par	36	Carts	$15	Clubs	$5

Roxbury

Shephard Hills Golf Assn. | Golf Course Rd. • Zip 12474

Phone	(607) 326-7121
Hours Open	Daylight hours
Average Green Fees	$11 - $15 wkdays, $15 - $19 wkends & holidays
Special Rates?	Call for details
Credit Cards	No
Season	Mid April - mid October
Amenities	Pro shop, bar, snack bar
Dress Code	No
Tee Time Required?	No
Golf Packages Available?	No
10% discount available?	Inquire

Validation _____ Score_____ Date _____

# of Holes	9	Par	36	Carts	$14	Clubs	NO

Stamford

Stamford Golf Club | Taylor Rd., PO Box 164 • Zip 12167

Phone	(607)652-7398
Hours Open	Daylight hours
Average Green Fees	$16 wkdays, $23 wkends & holidays
Special Rates?	No
Credit Cards	No
Season	April - October
Amenities	Pro shop, lessons, bar, restaurant, driving range
Dress Code	Proper golf attire, shirts w/sleeves
Tee Time Required?	No
Golf Packages Available?	No
10% discount available?	No

Validation _____ Score_____ Date _____

# of Holes	18	Par	70	Carts	YES	Clubs	YES

Fishkill

Fishkill Golf Course

RR 9 Box 594 • Zip 12524

Phone	(914) 896-5220
Hours Open	7 AM - dusk
Average Green Fees	$10 and under
Special Rates?	Senior citizens
Credit Cards	
Season	April 1 - December 1
Amenities	Pro shop, driving range
Dress Code	No
Tee Time Required?	No
Golf Packages Available?	No
10% discount available?	No

Validation _____ Score _____ Date _____

# of Holes	9	Par	29	Carts	YES	Clubs	$5

Hopewell Junction

Beekman Country Club

11 Country Club Rd. • Zip 12533

Phone	(914) 226-7700
Hours Open	Daylight hours
Average Green Fees	$16 - $22
Special Rates?	Please call for details
Credit Cards	No
Season	April - late November
Amenities	Pro shop, lessons, bar, restaurant, bucket or range balls w/greens fees
Dress Code	Yes
Tee Time Required?	Wkends
Golf Packages Available?	Lunch special, outings
10% discount available?	Inquire

Validation _____ Score _____ Date _____

# of Holes	3-9	Par	35/36/35	Carts	$29	Clubs	$5

Pawling

Dutcher Golf Course

E. Main • Zip 12564

Phone	(914) 855-9845
Hours Open	Daylight hours
Average Green Fees	$9 - $11 wkdays; $11 - $13 wkends
Special Rates?	After 4 PM $6; Senior citizens $8 - $10
Credit Cards	MC/VISA
Season	April - October
Amenities	Snack bar, pro shop, lessons
Dress Code	Proper golf attire
Tee Time Required?	No
Golf Packages Available?	No
10% discount available?	Yes

Validation _____ Score _____ Date _____

# of Holes	9	Par	34	Carts	$10/$15	Clubs	$5

Pine Plains

Thomas Carvel C. C.

Ferris Rd. off Taughanick St. • Zip 12567

Phone	(518) 398-7101
Hours Open	Daylight hours
Average Green Fees	$29
Special Rates?	Passes available during week
Credit Cards	MC/VISA
Season	April 15 - November 1
Amenities	Pro shop, lessons, bar, restaurant
Dress Code	Yes
Tee Time Required?	Yes
Golf Packages Available?	Yes
10% discount available?	Inquire

Validation _____ Score _____ Date _____

# of Holes	18	Par	73	Carts	INCL	Clubs	YES

Pleasant Valley

James Baird State Park

Freedom Plains Rd. • Zip 12569

Phone	(914) 452-1489
Hours Open	7 AM - dusk wkdays; 6 AM - dusk wkends & holidays
Average Green Fees	$12 and under
Special Rates?	Please call for details
Credit Cards	No
Season	April - November 1st
Amenities	Pro shop, lessons, bar, restaurant
Dress Code	Shirts, shoes required (sneakers okay)
Tee Time Required?	No (914)485-7358 for times & info
Golf Packages Available?	No
10% discount available?	No

Validation _____ Score _____ Date _____

# of Holes	18	Par	71	Carts	$19	Clubs	

Poughkeepsie

J. C. McCann Golf Course

Wilbur Blvd. • Zip 12603

Phone	(914) 454-1968
Hours Open	Daylight hours
Average Green Fees	$10 and under
Special Rates?	Wkdays
Credit Cards	
Season	
Amenities	Pro shop, lessons, bar, restaurant
Dress Code	Yes
Tee Time Required?	No
Golf Packages Available?	No
10% discount available?	No

Validation _____ Score _____ Date _____

# of Holes	18	Par	71	Carts	$15	Clubs	

Poughkeepsie

Vassar Golf Course

Raymond Ave. • Zip 12603

Phone	(914) 473-1550
Hours Open	8 AM - to dark
Average Green Fees	$10 and under
Special Rates?	Wkdays for senior citizens & juniors
Credit Cards	No
Season	April - November
Amenities	
Dress Code	Yes
Tee Time Required?	No
Golf Packages Available?	No
10% discount available?	No

Validation _____ Score _____ Date _____

# of Holes	9	Par	34	Carts	YES	Clubs	YES

Staatsburg

Dinsmore Golf Club

Rt. 9 • Zip 12580

Phone	(914) 889-4071
Hours Open	7 AM - dusk wkdays, 6 AM - dusk wkends
Average Green Fees	$10 and under
Special Rates?	Please call for details
Credit Cards	No
Season	May - September
Amenities	Pro shop, lessons, bar, restaurant, showers, locker
Dress Code	
Tee Time Required?	Call (914)889-3125 for tee times
Golf Packages Available?	No
10% discount available?	No

Validation _____ Score _____ Date _____

# of Holes	18	Par	70	Carts	$10-$20	Clubs	

Akron

Bright Meadows G.C.
12287 Clarence Center Rd. • Zip 14001

Phone	(716) 542-2441
Hours Open	Daylight hours
Average Green Fees	$5-Par 3($8/$10 reg. 9 wkends & holidays +$2
Special Rates?	$6.50/9wkdays(par 3-$4 Senior Citizens)
Credit Cards	No
Season	March - til (weather permitting)
Amenities	Driving range, snack bar, pro shop
Dress Code	Shirts
Tee Time Required?	Wkends
Golf Packages Available?	Yes
10% discount available?	Yes

Validation _____ Score _____ Date _____

# of Holes	9/9/9	Par	36	Carts	$8/$14	Clubs	$2.50

Akron

Dande Farms Golf Course
13278 Carney Rd. • Zip 14001

Phone	(716) 542-2027
Hours Open	Daylight hours
Average Green Fees	$14 wkdays, $17 wkends
Special Rates?	No
Credit Cards	
Season	2nd week April - 2nd week November
Amenities	Limited pro shop, full kitchen, practice green, putting green
Dress Code	Proper golf attire
Tee Time Required?	Wkends
Golf Packages Available?	Call for details
10% discount available?	Inquire

Validation _____ Score _____ Date _____

# of Holes	18	Par	71	Carts	$19	Clubs	$5

Angola

Grandview Golf Course

9211 Lake Shore Rd. • Zip 14006

Phone	(716) 549-4930
Hours Open	7 AM - dark
Average Green Fees	$10 and under
Special Rates?	Senior Citizens, groups
Credit Cards	No
Season	March - Mid October
Amenities	Limited pro shop, restaurant
Dress Code	No
Tee Time Required?	No
Golf Packages Available?	Yes
10% discount available?	Inquire

Validation _____ Score _____ Date _____

# of Holes	9	Par	33	Carts	YES	Clubs	YES

Buffalo

Cazenovia Park

Willink Ave. • Zip 14210

Phone	(716) 825-9811
Hours Open	Daylight hours
Average Green Fees	$8 - $10
Special Rates?	Senior Citizens, youth
Credit Cards	No
Season	
Amenities	Pro shop, lessons, food only
Dress Code	Proper dress required
Tee Time Required?	No
Golf Packages Available?	No
10% discount available?	No

Validation _____ Score _____ Date _____

# of Holes	9	Par	36	Carts	NO	Clubs	NO

Delaware Park
Parkside & Elmwood Ave. • Zip 14214

Phone	(716) 835-2533
Hours Open	Daylight hours
Average Green Fees	Res. $6 - $8, Non. Res. $10 - $12
Special Rates?	Senior Ctizens, youth
Credit Cards	No
Season	May - October
Amenities	Snack bar, refreshments
Dress Code	Proper dress required
Tee Time Required?	No
Golf Packages Available?	No
10% discount available?	No

Validation _____ Score _____ Date _____

# of Holes	18	Par	68	Carts	NO	Clubs	NO

Oakwood Golf Course
3575 Tonawanda Creek Rd. • Zip 14228

Phone	(716) 689-1421
Hours Open	Daylight hours
Average Green Fees	Res. $7 - $8, $14 wkends & holidays
Special Rates?	Inquire
Credit Cards	No
Season	April - November
Amenities	Limited pro shop, candy & snacks
Dress Code	Shirts required
Tee Time Required?	No
Golf Packages Available?	No
10% discount available?	Inquire

Validation _____ Score _____ Date _____

# of Holes	9	Par	35	Carts	PULL	Clubs	YES

Buffalo

South Park
South Park & McKinley Pkwy. • Zip 14218

Phone	(716) 825-9504
Hours Open	Daylight hours
Average Green Fees	$8 - $10
Special Rates?	Senior Citizens, youth
Credit Cards	No
Season	
Amenities	Yes
Dress Code	Proper dress required
Tee Time Required?	No
Golf Packages Available?	No
10% discount available?	No

Validation _____ Score_____ Date _____

# of Holes	9	Par	35	Carts	NO	Clubs	NO

Cheektowaga

Birdies & Bogies
Gallerian Mall Suite S101 2000Walden Ave. • Zip 14225

Phone	(716) 684-0346
Hours Open	10 AM - 10 PM (Monday-Saturday)
	11 AM - 7 PM (Sundays)
Average Green Fees	$5.50 Adults, $4 under 10 & Senior Citizens
Special Rates?	Group rates, tournaments
Credit Cards	MC/VISA
Season	All Year
Amenities	Indoor golf simulators, vending machines, remote control boats in water ($1off/round miniature golf w/book)
Dress Code	Shirts & shoes required
Tee Time Required?	On simulators
Golf Packages Available?	Call for details
10% discount available?	Inquire

Validation _____ Score_____ Date _____

# of Holes	18	Par	51	Carts	NO	Clubs	$5

Clarence

Pine Meadows G & C

9820 Greiner Rd. • Zip 14031

Phone	(716) 741-3970
Hours Open	Daylight hours
Average Green Fees	$6 - $10
Special Rates?	Senior Citizens on Tues. till 12 PM $1 off
Credit Cards	No
Season	May 1 - October
Amenities	Limited pro shop, snacks
Dress Code	Shirts required
Tee Time Required?	No
Golf Packages Available?	No
10% discount available?	Yes

Validation _____ Score_____ Date _____

# of Holes	9	Par	66	Carts	$10/$12	Clubs	$3

Clarence Center

Greenwood Golf Course

8499 Northfield Rd. • Zip 14032

Phone	(716)741-3395
Hours Open	7 AM - 10 PM
Average Green Fees	$6.50/$8.50 wkdays, $8/$10.50 wkends
Special Rates?	Senior citizens
Credit Cards	No
Season	April - October
Amenities	Snack bar, alcoholic beverages
Dress Code	Shirts & shoes must be worn in building
Tee Time Required?	No
Golf Packages Available?	No
10% discount available?	No

Validation _____ Score_____ Date _____

# of Holes	9	Par	36	Carts	$8/$14	Clubs	$2

Colden

Hidden Acres Golf Course

Route 240 • Zip 14033

Phone	(716) 941-9034
Hours Open	7 AM - 9 PM
Average Green Fees	$4/$7 wkdays, $5/$8 wkends & holidays
Special Rates?	Mondays for Senior Citizens $3/$6
Credit Cards	No
Season	Mid April - November 1
Amenities	Lessons
Dress Code	No street shoes
Tee Time Required?	No
Golf Packages Available?	No
10% discount available?	Yes

Validation _____ Score_____ Date _____

# of Holes	18	Par	72	Carts	INCL	Clubs	$10

East Amherst

Glen Oak Golf Course

711 Smith Rd. • E. Amherst 14051

Phone	(716)688-5454
Hours Open	Daylight hours
Average Greens Fees	$29 wkdays, $40 wkends
Special Rates?	Senior citizens $16 before 9 AM
Credit Cards	MC/VISA
Season	April 1 - December 1
Amenities	Pro shop, lessons, bar, restaurant, putting green, driving range
Dress Code	Collared shirts, no cutoffs or tanktops
Tee Time Required?	Yes 3 days in advance
Golf Packages Available?	No
10% discount available?	Inquire

Validation _____ Score_____ Date _____

# of Holes	18	Par	72	Carts	INCL	Clubs	$10

Eden

Eden Valley Golf Course

10401 Sisson Hwy. • Zip 14057

Phone	(716) 337-2190
Hours Open	Daylight hours
Average Green Fees	$6 - $9 wkdays, $8 - $12 wkends
Special Rates?	No
Credit Cards	No
Season	April - October
Amenities	Restaurant, snack bar, pro shop
Dress Code	Proper golf attire
Tee Time Required?	Saturdays
Golf Packages Available?	Inquire
10% discount available?	Inquire

Validation_____Score_____Date_____

# of Holes	18	Par	72	Carts	YES	Clubs	YES

Elma

Elma Meadows G.C.

1711 Gridle Rd. • Zip 14059

Phone	(716) 652-5475
Hours Open	Daylight hours
Average Green Fees	$11 wkdays, $13 wkends
Special Rates?	
Credit Cards	
Season	
Amenities	Pro shop, lessons, food
Dress Code	Casual
Tee Time Required?	No
Golf Packages Available?	No
10% discount available?	No

Validation_____Score_____Date_____

# of Holes	18	Par	70	Carts	$16	Clubs	

Glenwood

Holland Hills C.C.

10438 Holland & Greenwood Rd. • Zip 14069

Phone	(716) 537-2345
Hours Open	Daylight hours
Average Green Fees	$13 wkdays, $15 wkends
Special Rates?	After 5 PM - $7
Credit Cards	
Season	May 1 - October 31
Amenities	Pro shop, bar, restaurant w/soup & sandwiches, Friday night dinners
Dress Code	Minimal
Tee Time Required?	Yes
Golf Packages Available?	No
10% discount available?	Inquire

Validation_____Score_____Date_____

# of Holes	18	Par	72	Carts	$15	Clubs	$7

Grand Island

Beaver Island G.C.

2136 W. Oakfield Rd. • Zip 14072

Phone	(716) 773-3271
Hours Open	6 AM - dark
Average Green Fees	$10 - $20
Special Rates?	Senior Citizens
Credit Cards	
Season	Mid April - 1st week in November
Amenities	Pro shop, lessons, restaurant
Dress Code	Shirts must be worn
Tee Time Required?	Wkends; call 773-4150 Thursday, 9 AM - noon for Saturday, Friday, 9 AM - noon for Sunday
Golf Packages Available?	No
10% discount available?	No

Validation_____Score_____Date_____

# of Holes	18	Par	74	Carts	YES	Clubs	YES

Grand Island

River Oaks Golf Club

201 Whitehaven Rd. • Zip 14072

Phone	(716) 773-3336
Hours Open	7 AM - 8 PM wkdays, 6 AM - 8 PM wkends
Average Green Fees	$22 - $28
Special Rates?	
Credit Cards	Yes
Season	
Amenities	Pro shop, lessons, bar, restaurant, showers
Dress Code	Yes
Tee Time Required?	Recommended
Golf Packages Available?	No
10% discount available?	No

Validation_____Score_____Date_____

# of Holes	18	Par	72	Carts	YES	Clubs	YES

Hamburg

South Shore C. C.

5076 Southwestern Blvd. • Zip 14075

Phone	(716) 649-6674
Hours Open	7 AM - 7 PM
Average Green Fees	$12/$20 wkdays, $22 wkends & holidays
Special Rates?	Senior Citizens wkdays $18/$25 with cart
Credit Cards	MC/VISA/DINERS
Season	April - October
Amenities	Pro shop, lessons, bar, restaurant
Dress Code	Proper golf attire
Tee Time Required?	Recommended
Golf Packages Available?	No
10% discount available?	Inquire

Validation_____Score_____Date_____

# of Holes	18	Par	72	Carts	$20	Clubs	$10

NorthAmherst

Evergreen Golf Club
100 Tonawanda Creek Rd. • Zip 14228

Phone	((716) 688-6204
Hours Open	Daylight hours
Average Green Fees	$6.50
Special Rates?	Senior Citizens
Credit Cards	No
Season	April 15 - November
Amenities	None
Dress Code	No
Tee Time Required?	No
Golf Packages Available?	No
10% discount available?	Yes

Validation_____ Score_____ Date_____

# of Holes	9	Par	36	Carts	$7.25	Clubs	$1.50

Orchard Park

Bob-O-Link Golf Club
54085 Transit Rd. • Zip 14127

Phone	(716) 662-4311
Hours Open	6 AM - 2 AM - Lights for night play
Average Green Fees	$10 and under
Special Rates?	Call for details
Credit Cards	No
Season	April - October
Amenities	None
Dress Code	Shirts
Tee Time Required?	No
Golf Packages Available?	No
10% discount available?	No

Validation_____ Score_____ Date_____

# of Holes	18	Par	3	Carts	YES	Clubs	$5

Brighton Park G.C.

Brompton Rd.• Zip 14150

Phone	(716) 875-8721
Hours Open	6 AM - 8 PM
Average Green Fees	$14
Special Rates?	Senior Citizens, town residents
Credit Cards	No
Season	May 1 - 1st week in November
Amenities	Snack shop, driving range
Dress Code	Shirts must be worn at all times
Tee Time Required?	No
Golf Packages Available?	No
10% discount available?	Inquire

Validation_____Score_____Date_____

# of Holes	18	Par	72	Carts	$10/$16	Clubs	NO

Sheridan Park G. C.

Sheridan Dr. • Zip 14150

Phone	(716) 875-8721
Hours Open	6 AM - 8 PM
Average Green Fees	$14
Special Rates?	Senior Citizens, town residents
Credit Cards	No
Season	May 1 - 1st week in November
Amenities	Snack shop
Dress Code	Shirts must be worn at all times
Tee Time Required?	No
Golf Packages Available?	No
10% discount available?	No

Validation_____Score_____Date_____

# of Holes	18	Par	71	Carts	$10/$16	Clubs	NO

Williamsville

Amherst Audubon G.C.

500 Maple Rd. • Zip 14221

Phone	(716) 631-7139
Hours Open	Daylight hours
Average Green Fees	Res. $8 - $9, Non. Res. $15 - $19
Special Rates?	For seniors & residents
Credit Cards	MC/VISA
Season	2nd week April - Election Day
Amenities	Pro shop, lessons, bar, lunch counter, putting green
Dress Code	Shirts must be worn at all times
Tee Time Required?	No, but available
Golf Packages Available?	No
10% discount available?	Inquire

Validation_____Score_____Date_____

# of Holes	18	Par	71	Carts	$17	Clubs	$8

Williamsville

Audubon Par-3 Golf Course

475 Maple Rd. • Zip 14221

Phone	(716) 631-7124
Hours Open	Daylight hours
Average Green Fees	Res. $3 - $4, Non. Res. $6 - $8
Special Rates?	Seniors on Wed. $2 w/cart
Credit Cards	No
Season	April - Election Day
Amenities	Pro shop, lessons, food, electric carts available across street
Dress Code	No
Tee Time Required?	No
Golf Packages Available?	Inquire
10% discount available?	Inquire

Validation_____Score_____Date_____

# of Holes	9	Par	27	Carts	YES	Clubs	$8

AuSable Forks

Ausable Valley G.C.
Golf Course Rd.• Zip 12912

Phone	(518) 647-8666
Hours Open	8 AM - 8 PM
Average Green Fees	$10 and under
Special Rates?	
Credit Cards	Anticipated
Season	April 1 - October 31
Amenities	Practice green, lessons, pro shop, meals
Dress Code	
Tee Time Required?	
Golf Packages Available?	
10% discount available?	Inquire

Validation_____Score_____Date_____

# of Holes	9	Par	34	Carts	$15	Clubs	YES

Elizabethtown

Cobble Hill Golf Course
High Street • Zip 12932

Phone	(518) 873-9974
Hours Open	8 AM - 8 PM
Average Green Fees	$10 daily
Special Rates?	$35 for 5 days
Credit Cards	No
Season	April 15 - October 1
Amenities	Food bar
Dress Code	Fully dressed
Tee Time Required?	No
Golf Packages Available?	No
10% discount available?	No

Validation_____Score_____Date_____

# of Holes	9	Par	34	Carts	$8/$14	Clubs	$4

Lake Placid

Craig Wood Golf & C.C.

Cascade Rd. • Zip 12946

Phone	(518) 523-9811
Hours Open	7 AM - dusk
Average Green Fees	$16
Special Rates?	
Credit Cards	MC/VISA
Season	May 15 - November 1
Amenities	Restaurant, bar
Dress Code	Yes
Tee Time Required?	Yes
Golf Packages Available?	No
10% discount available?	No

Validation_____ Score_____ Date_____

# of Holes	18	Par	72	Carts	YES	Clubs	YES

Lake Placid

Whiteface Inn Resort & Club

PO Box 231 • Zip 12946

Phone	(518)523-2551 Ext. 116
Hours Open	7:30 AM - 6 PM
Average Green Fees	$24 wkdays, $29 wkends
Special Rates?	Early Season 5/15 to 6/15
Credit Cards	AMEX/MC/VISA/DISC
Season	
Amenities	Practice greens, chipping area
Dress Code	Conservative dress required
Tee Time Required?	Yes
Golf Packages Available?	Yes
10% discount available?	Yes

Validation_____ Score_____ Date_____

# of Holes	18	Par	72	Carts	$24/$26	Clubs	$10

Port Henry

Moriah
Broad St. • Zip 12974

Phone	(518) 546-9979
Hours Open	Dawn to dark
Average Green Fees	$12 all day, after 5 PM $8
Special Rates?	$35 for 2 people w/cart
Credit Cards	MC/VISA
Season	End of April - October
Amenities	Bar, limited pro shop, snacks
Dress Code	Shirts required
Tee Time Required?	No
Golf Packages Available?	No
10% discount available?	Inquire

Validation_____Score_____Date_____

# of Holes	9	Par	32	Carts	YES	Clubs	NO

Ray Brook

Saranac Lake Golf Club
Rt. 86 • Zip 12977

Phone	(518) 891-2675
Hours Open	7 AM - dusk
Average Green Fees	$15
Special Rates?	After 4 PM
Credit Cards	No
Season	May 1 - December 15
Amenities	Driving range, lounge, putting green
Dress Code	No
Tee Time Required?	No
Golf Packages Available?	No
10% discount available?	No

Validation_____Score_____Date_____

# of Holes	9	Par	36	Carts	$18	Clubs	$5

Schroon Lake

Town of Schroon G.C.
Hoffman Rd. • Zip 12870

Phone	(518) 532-9359
Hours Open	Daylight hours
Average Green Fees	$11
Special Rates?	No
Credit Cards	No
Season	May - October
Amenities	Pro shop, snack bar
Dress Code	Shirts must be worn at all times
Tee Time Required?	No
Golf Packages Available?	No
10% discount available?	Inquire

Validation_____Score_____Date_____

# of Holes	9	Par	36	Carts	$10/$18	Clubs	YES

Westport

Westport Country Club
Liberty St. • Zip 12993

Phone	(518) 962-4470
Hours Open	Daylight hours
Average Green Fees	$25
Special Rates?	Yes
Credit Cards	MC/VISA
Season	April 15 - October 15
Amenities	Pro shop, lessons, bar, restaurant
Dress Code	Casual
Tee Time Required?	Yes
Golf Packages Available?	Yes
10% discount available?	Inquire

Validation_____Score_____Date_____

# of Holes	18	Par	72	Carts	YES	Clubs	YES

Willsboro Golf Club
Point Rd. PO Box 605 • Zip 12996

Phone	(518) 963-8989
Hours Open	Daylight hours
Average Green Fees	$10 - $12
Special Rates?	Call for details
Credit Cards	No
Season	April - November (weather permitting)
Amenities	Pro shop, food nearby
Dress Code	No halters, short shorts
Tee Time Required?	No
Golf Packages Available?	No
10% discount available?	Yes

Validation_____Score_____Date_____

# of Holes	9	Par	35	Carts	YES	Clubs	YES

Loon Lake

Loon Lake Golf Course

Rt. 99 • Zip 12968

Phone	(518) 891-3249
Hours Open	7 AM - dark
Average Green Fees	$14
Special Rates?	After 4 PM - 1/2 price
Credit Cards	No
Season	April 15 - September 30
Amenities	Practice range, pro shop, putting green, restaurant for lunch & continental breakfasts
Dress Code	Proper golf attire
Tee Time Required?	Wkends & holidays
Golf Packages Available?	Saranac Hotel w/meals & unlimited golf
10% discount available?	No

Validation_____Score_____Date_____

# of Holes	18	Par	70	Carts	$16	Clubs	$5

Malone

Malone Golf Club

Whippleville Rd. • Zip 12953

Phone	(518) 483-2926
Hours Open	Daylight hours
Average Green Fees	$24
Special Rates?	
Credit Cards	MC/VISA
Season	April 15 - October 31
Amenities	Practice green, lessons, pro shop, meals available
Dress Code	Yes
Tee Time Required?	Daily
Golf Packages Available?	Yes
10% discount available?	No

Validation_____Score_____Date_____

# of Holes	18/18	Par	72/71	Carts	$22	Clubs	YES

Saranac Lake

Saranac Inn Golf & C. C.   Rt. 30 • Zip 12983

Phone	(518) 891-1402
Hours Open	8 AM - 3 PM
Average Green Fees	$45
Special Rates?	No
Credit Cards	MC/VISA
Season	May 15 - October 15
Amenities	Bar, restaurant, pro shop, lessons, putting green, driving range
Dress Code	Proper golf attire
Tee Time Required?	Suggested
Golf Packages Available?	Yes
10% discount available?	No

Validation_____Score_____Date_____

# of Holes	18	Par	72	Carts	INCL	Clubs	YES

Tupper Lake

Tupper Lake Golf & C. C.   Country Club Rd. •Zip 12986

Phone	(518) 359-3701
Hours Open	7:30 AM - 7:30 PM
Average Green Fees	$10 - $20
Special Rates?	9 holes rate, off season rate
Credit Cards	No
Season	May - October 1
Amenities	Practice green, lessons, pro shop, meals available
Dress Code	
Tee Time Required?	
Golf Packages Available?	
10% discount available?	Inquire

Validation_____Score_____Date_____

# of Holes	18	Par	71	Carts	$15-$25	Clubs	YES

Caroga Lake

Nick Stoner Golf Course

Hwy. 29A & Rt. 10 • Zip 12032

Phone	(518) 835-4220
Hours Open	Daylight hours
Average Green Fees	$9.50 wkdays, $12 wkends
Special Rates?	No
Credit Cards	No
Season	May 1 - October 31
Amenities	Pro shop, lessons
Dress Code	
Tee Time Required?	No, suggest call on tournaments
Golf Packages Available?	No
10% discount available?	Inquire

Validation_____Score_____Date_____

# of Holes	18	Par	70	Carts	$17	Clubs	$7

Gloversville

Holland Meadows G.C.

RD #2 State Hwy. 29 • Zip 12078

Phone	(518883-3318
Hours Open	Daylight hours
Average Green Fees	$5/9, $10 greens
Special Rates?	Senior Citizens
Credit Cards	MC/VISA/DISC
Season	April 1 - November 1
Amenities	Pro shop, lessons, driving range
Dress Code	No
Tee Time Required?	No
Golf Packages Available?	No
10% discount available?	Yes

Validation_____Score_____Date_____

# of Holes	EXEC 18	Par	59	Carts	$12	Clubs	$5

Gloversville

Kingsboro Golf Club, Inc.
301 N. Kingsboro Ave. • Zip 12078

Phone	(518) 773-4600
Hours Open	Daylight hours
Average Green Fees	$8 - $10 (after 4 PM wkdays - $6.50)
Special Rates?	Senior Citizens
Credit Cards	MC/VISA
Season	April 15 - November 15
Amenities	Restaurant, bar
Dress Code	No
Tee Time Required?	No
Golf Packages Available?	No
10% discount available?	Inquire

Validation_____Score_____Date_____

# of Holes	9	Par	73	Carts	$10/$16	Clubs	$5

Johnstown

Alban Hills Country Club
Alban Hills Dr. •Zip 12095

Phone	(518) 762-3717
Hours Open	Daylight hours
Average Green Fees	$12 - $14
Special Rates?	Senior Citizens
Credit Cards	No
Season	April 15 - November
Amenities	Restaurant, bar, lounge, putting green, pro shop
Dress Code	Yes
Tee Time Required?	No
Golf Packages Available?	No
10% discount available?	Inquire

Validation_____Score_____Date_____

# of Holes	18	Par	70	Carts	YES	Clubs	YES

Northville

Sacandaga Golf Club

Sacandaga Park • Zip 12134

Phone	(518) 863-4887
Hours Open	7 AM - 9 PM
Average Green Fees	$10 and under
Special Rates?	Call for details
Credit Cards	No
Season	Early April - Early November
Amenities	Pro shop, lessons, bar, restaurant
Dress Code	Yes
Tee Time Required?	No
Golf Packages Available?	No
10% discount available?	Yes

Validation_____Score_____Date_____

# of Holes	9	Par	36	Carts	YES	Clubs	$5

Batavia Country Club
7909 Batavia-Byron Rd. • Zip 14020

Phone	(716) 343-7600
Hours Open	6 AM - 9 PM
Average Green Fees	$8/$10 wkdays, $10/$13 wkends
Special Rates?	Call for details
Credit Cards	MC/VISA
Season	April - October
Amenities	Pro shop, bar, restaurant, driving range
Dress Code	Shirts w/collars
Tee Time Required?	Yes
Golf Packages Available?	Yes
10% discount available?	No

Validation_____Score_____Date_____

# of Holes	18	Par	72	Carts	YES	Clubs	$5

Terry Hills Golf Course
Rt. 33(1mi.E. of Batavia) • Zip 14020

Phone	(716) 343-0860 or (800) 825-8633
Hours Open	Daylight hours
Average Green Fees	$10 - $20
Special Rates?	Wkdays
Credit Cards	All
Season	April 1 - November 1
Amenities	Pro shop, lessons, bar, restaurant, driving range, putting green, miniature golf, pavilion for parties
Dress Code	No
Tee Time Required?	Recommended May - October
Golf Packages Available?	Yes
10% discount available?	No

Validation_____Score_____Date_____

# of Holes	18	Par	72	Carts	$9	Clubs	$5-$10

Darien

Chestnut Hill Golf Course
1330 Broadway Rd. • Zip 14040

Phone	(716) 547-3613
Hours Open	Daylight hours
Average Green Fees	$20 wkdays, $25 wkends & holidays
Special Rates?	Senior Citizens ($16 wkdays)
Credit Cards	VISA / AMEX
Season	April 15 - December
Amenities	Pro shop, lessons, bar, restaurant
Dress Code	No short shorts
Tee Time Required?	Recommended
Golf Packages Available?	Yes
10% discount available?	No

Validation_____Score_____Date_____

# of Holes	18	Par	72	Carts	INCL	Clubs	$5

LeRoy

LeRoy Country Club
7759 E. Main St. • Zip 14482

Phone	(716) 768-7330
Hours Open	Daylight hours
Average Green Fees	$14
Special Rates?	Call for details
Credit Cards	MC / VISA
Season	April 1 - October 31
Amenities	Pro shop, lessons, bar, restaurant, swimming pool, driving range, locker rooms
Dress Code	Collared shirt
Tee Time Required?	Wkends & Holidays
Golf Packages Available?	Call for details
10% discount available?	Inquire

Validation_____Score_____Date_____

# of Holes	18	Par	71	Carts	$18	Clubs	$5

Stafford

Carter's Sweetland Pines

5795 Sweetland Rd. • Zip 14143

Phone	(716) 343-7059
Hours Open	7 AM - dark
Average Green Fees	$5 - $10
Special Rates?	Early bird wkdays (7 AM - noon) $4
Credit Cards	No
Season	April - November 1
Amenities	
Dress Code	Shirts
Tee Time Required?	No
Golf Packages Available?	Yes
10% discount available?	Yes

Validation_____Score_____Date_____

# of Holes	9	Par	27	Carts	PULL	Clubs	YES

Freehold

Pleasant View Lodge & Golf

Gayhead Rd. • Zip 12431

Phone	(518) 634-2523
Hours Open	8 AM - 5 PM
Average Green Fees	$14
Special Rates?	No
Credit Cards	MC/VISA/DISC
Season	April - ?
Amenities	Pro shop, lessons, bar, restaurant, driving range
Dress Code	No tank tops, cutoffs
Tee Time Required?	Yes
Golf Packages Available?	Yes
10% discount available?	Inquire

Validation_____Score_____Date_____

# of Holes	9	Par	36	Carts	YES	Clubs	YES

Greenville

Rainbow Golf Course

Rt. 26 • Zip 12083

Phone	(518) 966-5343
Hours Open	7:30 AM - dusk
Average Green Fees	$10 - $20
Special Rates?	
Credit Cards	
Season	
Amenities	Pro shop, lessons, bar, restaurant, driving range
Dress Code	
Tee Time Required?	Yes 24 hours notice
Golf Packages Available?	Yes-for lodging all guests play free golf
10% discount available?	Yes

Validation_____Score_____Date_____

# of Holes	9	Par	36	Carts	YES

Greenville

Sunny Hill Golf Course

Sunny Hill Rd. • Zip 12083

Phone	(518) 634-7642
Hours Open	Daylight hours
Average Green Fees	$11 wkdays, $12 wkends
Special Rates?	Senior Citizens, group rates
Credit Cards	No
Season	Early April - November 1
Amenities	Snack bar, club house, full service resort w/meals included daily
Dress Code	Shirts & shoes must be worn at all times
Tee Time Required?	No
Golf Packages Available?	Yes call for details
10% discount available?	Inquire

Validation_____Score_____Date_____

# of Holes	18	Par	66	Carts	$10/$17	Clubs	$5

Palenville

Rip Van Winkle G.C.

Rt. 23A • Zip 12463

Phone	(518) 678-9779
Hours Open	7 AM - dark
Average Green Fees	$12 wkdays, $15 wkends & holidays
Special Rates?	After 4 PM M - F $9
Credit Cards	No
Season	April 1 - mid November
Amenities	Pro shop, lessons, bar, restaurant, semi-private, memberships
Dress Code	No tank tops
Tee Time Required?	No, available on wkends
Golf Packages Available?	No
10% discount available?	Yes

Validation_____Score_____Date_____

# of Holes	9	Par	36	Carts	YES	Clubs	$6

Tannersville

Colonial Golf Course

Main St. • Zip 12485

Phone	(518) 589-9807
Hours Open	Daylight hours
Average Green Fees	$10 - $20
Special Rates?	
Credit Cards	
Season	
Amenities	Pro shop, bar, restaurant
Dress Code	
Tee Time Required?	
Golf Packages Available?	
10% discount available?	Inquire

Validation_____Score_____Date_____

# of Holes	9	Par	35	Carts	YES

Windham

Windham Golf Course

South St. • Zip 12496

Phone	(518) 734-9910
Hours Open	Daylight hours
Average Green Fees	$21 wkdays, $26 wkends
Special Rates?	Senior Citizens M-F $13. After 4 PM $13
Credit Cards	MC/VISA
Season	April 1 - October 31
Amenities	Pro shop, lessons, bar, restaurant
Dress Code	Proper golf attire
Tee Time Required?	Highly recommended
Golf Packages Available?	No
10% discount available?	No

Validation_____Score_____Date_____

# of Holes	18	Par	71	Carts	$22-$24	Clubs	$15

Indian Lake

Cedar River Golf Course
Rt. 28 & 30 • Zip 12842

Phone	(518) 648-5906
Hours Open	Daylight hours
Average Green Fees	$8 - $12
Special Rates?	
Credit Cards	No
Season	Memorial Day - Columbus Day
Amenities	Pro shop, lessons, bar, restaurant
Dress Code	
Tee Time Required?	No
Golf Packages Available?	No
10% discount available?	No

Validation_____Score_____Date_____

# of Holes	9	Par	36	Carts	$8/$14	Clubs	$4

Indian Lake

Wakely Lodge & Golf Course
110 Cedar River Rd. • Zip 12842

Phone	(518) 648-5011
Hours Open	7 AM - dark
Average Green Fees	$10 - $20
Special Rates?	
Credit Cards	
Season	May 1 - November 1 (weather permitting)
Amenities	Bar, restaurant, pro shop, gift shop
Dress Code	Proper shoes & shirts
Tee Time Required?	No
Golf Packages Available?	Groups only by prior arrangements
10% discount available?	Inquire

Validation_____Score_____Date_____

# of Holes	9	Par	34	Carts	YES	Clubs	YES

Inlet Golf Club
Rt. 28 • Zip 13360

Phone	(315) 357-3503
Hours Open	7 AM to dark
Average Green Fees	$10 - $20 wkdays
Special Rates?	Group rates
Credit Cards	No
Season	April 25 - October 15
Amenities	Pro shop, lessons
Dress Code	Must wear shirt at all times
Tee Time Required?	No
Golf Packages Available?	10 play tickets available
10% discount available?	Yes

Validation_____Score_____Date_____

# of Holes	18	Par	70	Carts'	YES	Clubs	YES

Lake Pleasant Golf Inc.
RR 8, Box 709 • Zip 12108

Phone	(518) 548-7071
Hours Open	Daylight hours
Average Green Fees	$12
Special Rates?	No
Credit Cards	No
Season	May - September
Amenities	Pro shop, lessons
Dress Code	Shirts and shoes required
Tee Time Required?	Wkends
Golf Packages Available?	No
10% discount available?	Inquire

Validation_____Score_____Date_____

# of Holes	9	Par	35	Carts	$8.50/$17	Clubs	$7.50

Frankfort

Grygiel's Pine Hills G.C.

Jones Rd. • Zip 13340

Phone	(315) 894-3970
Hours Open	Daylight hours
Average Green Fees	$9 weekdays, $11 weekends/holidays
Special Rates?	No
Credit Cards	No
Season	April 15- October 31
Amenities	Pro Shop, lessons, bar, restaurant
Dress Code	No
Tee Time Required?	1st come, 1st served
Golf Packages Available?	No
10% discount available?	Yes

Validation_____ Score_____ Date_____

# of Holes	18	Par	70	Carts	$8 and $16	Clubs	$5 - all day

Frankfort

Maple Creek G.C.

Upper Barringer Rd. • Zip 13340

Phone	(315) 894-3970
Hours Open	Daylight hours
Average Green Fees	$10 and under
Special Rates?	Senior Citizens on membership only
Credit Cards	No
Season	April - October
Amenities	Driving range, snack shop, alcoholic beverages, pro shop
Dress Code	Shirts and shoes must be worn at all times
Tee Time Required?	No
Golf Packages Available?	No
10% discount available?	No

Validation_____ Score_____ Date_____

# of Holes	9	Par	35	Carts	YES	Clubs	$3.75

Doty's Golf Course   RD #1, Barringer Rd. • Zip 13357

Phone	(315) 894-2860
Hours Open	Wkdays 8 AM - dusk, wkends 7 AM - dusk
Average Green Fees	$7/9 holes, $12/18 holes
Special Rates?	No
Credit Cards	No
Season	April 1 - November
Amenities	Limited pro shop, lessons, vending machines
Dress Code	Proper golf attire
Tee Time Required?	No, but available
Golf Packages Available?	No
10% discount available?	No

Validation_____Score_____Date_____

# of Holes	9	Par	35	Carts	YES	Clubs	

Little Falls Golf Course   Rt. 170 • Fairfield Rd. • Zip 13365

Phone	(315) 823-4442
Hours Open	8am-6pm (April and October)
	7am-9pm (May - September)
Average Green Fees	$7 weekdays - $8 weekends/holidays
Special Rates?	
Credit Cards	
Season	April-October
Amenities	Pro Shop, bar, snack shop
Dress Code	Shirts must be worn
Tee Time Required?	No
Golf Packages Available?	No
10% discount available?	Yes

Validation_____Score_____Date_____

# of Holes	9	Par	36	Carts	SEE MGR.	Clubs	

Little Falls

Mohawk Valley Golf Course
Rt. 5 • Zip 13416

Phone	(315) 866-0204
Hours Open	Daylight hours
Average Green Fees	$7.50 and $12
Special Rates?	No
Credit Cards	No
Season	April 15-October (weather permitting)
Amenities	Pro shop, lessons, bar, restaurant, driving range, swimming pool, tennis courts
Dress Code	No tanktops
Tee Time Required?	Suggested on weekends
Golf Packages Available?	Tues.- Ladies' Day, closed 9-1,Wed.- Men's Day
10% discount available?	Inquire closed 11-4

Validation_____Score_____Date_____

# of Holes	9	Par	36	Carts	No	Clubs	No

Newport

Golf Club of Newport
Honeyhill Rd. • Zip 13416

Phone	(315) 845-833
Hours Open	7am - dark
Average Green Fees	$11 wkdays, $13 wkends, holidays
Special Rates?	Please call for details
Credit Cards	No
Season	May 1- October 15
Amenities	Pro shop, lessons, bar, restaurant
Dress Code	Yes
Tee Time Required?	1 day in advance
Golf Packages Available?	No
10% discount available?	Inquire

Validation_____Score_____Date_____

# of Holes	18	Par	72	Carts	$18	Clubs	Yes

Thendara

Thendara Golf Club., Inc.

Rt. 28 • Zip 13472

Phone	(315) 369-3136
Hours Open	Daylight hours
Average Green Fees	$18
Special Rates?	No
Credit Cards	No
Season	May 1- October 15
Amenities	Pro Shop, lessons, bar, restaurant
Dress Code	Yes
Tee Time Required?	1 day in advance
Golf Packages Available?	No
10% discount available?	Inquire

Validation_____Score_____Date_____

# of Holes	18	Par	72	Carts	$18	Clubs	Yes

Adams

Tomacy's G.C. & Restaurant

Rt 11 • Zip 13605

Phone	(315) 232-4842
Hours Open	6:30 AM - 8 PM
Average Green Fees	$8/$12
Special Rates?	Group rates available
Credit Cards	MC/VISA
Season	April 1 - November 1
Amenities	Pro Shop, lessons, bar, restaurant practice range
Dress Code	
Tee Time Required?	No
Golf Packages Available?	
10% discount available?	No

Validation_____Score_____Date_____

# of Holes	9	Par	35	Carts	$7 & $14	Clubs	$3

Alexandria Bay

1000 Islands Golf Club

Wellesley Island E. • Zip 13607

Phone	(315) 482-9454
Hours Open	6:30 AM - 7:30 PM
Average Green Fees	$20 - $30
Special Rates?	No
Credit Cards	VISA/MC/AMEX
Season	April 15 - November 1
Amenities	Pro shop, lessons, bar, restaurant
Dress Code	No
Tee Time Required?	Yes
Golf Packages Available?	Yes
10% discount available?	No

Validation_____Score_____Date_____

# of Holes	18	Par	72	Carts	$10	Clubs	$6

Alexandria Bay

Oak Ridge Golf Club, Inc.

PO Box 391A • Zip 13607

Phone	(315) 482-3470
Hours Open	Daylight hours
Average Green Fees	$16.50
Special Rates?	After 3 PM
Credit Cards	MC/VISA
Season	Spring-Fall(Peak season July 1-Labor Day)
Amenities	
Dress Code	Shirt w/collar and sleeves, no cutoffs or jeans
Tee Time Required?	Yes
Golf Packages Available?	Yes
10% discount available?	Yes

Validation_____Score_____Date_____

# of Holes	18	Par	74	Carts	$18	Clubs	$5

Clayton

C-Way Golf Club

RR1 Box 271 • Zip 13624

Phone	(315) 686-4562
Hours Open	Daylight hours
Average Green Fees	$10 - $20 wkdays
Special Rates?	Group rates available
Credit Cards	MC/VISA
Season	May 1 - October
Amenities	Pro Shop, lessons, bar, restaurant
Dress Code	Shirts and shoes must be worn at all times
Tee Time Required?	Yes
Golf Packages Available?	Yes
10% discount available?	Inquire

Validation_____Score_____Date_____

# of Holes	18	Par	71	Carts	$16	Clubs	Yes

Clayton

Clayton Golf Club

Outer State St. Box 404 • Zip 13624

Phone	(315) 686-4242
Hours Open	Daylight hours
Average Green Fees	$7 - $10.50
Special Rates?	No
Credit Cards	No
Season	May - October
Amenities	Pro shop, lessons, bar, snack bar
Dress Code	No
Tee Time Required?	No
Golf Packages Available?	No
10% discount available?	YES

Validation_____Score_____Date_____

# of Holes	9	Par	35	Carts	$6/$11	Clubs	$3

Dexter

Rustic Golf and Country Club

Middle Rd. • Zip 13634

Phone	(315) 639-6800
Hours Open	Daylight hours
Average Green Fees	$8 - $13
Special Rates?	Please call for details
Credit Cards	No
Season	Mid April - October
Amenities	Pro shop, bar, restaurant
Dress Code	Shirts must be worn at all times
Tee Time Required?	No
Golf Packages Available?	No
10% discount available?	Yes

Validation_____Score_____Date_____

# of Holes	9	Par	30	Carts	Yes	Clubs	Yes

Mannsville

Lakeview Golf Course

Rt. 11 • Zip 13661

Phone	(315) 465-6516
Hours Open	Daylight hours
Average Green Fees	$5
Special Rates?	No
Credit Cards	No
Season	April/November (weather permitting)
Amenities	Limited pro shop
Dress Code	Shirts must be worn at all times, casual wear
Tee Time Required?	No
Golf Packages Available?	No
10% discount available?	No

Validation_____Score_____Date_____

# of Holes	9	Par	30	Carts	PULL	Clubs	$2.50

Sackets Harbor

Bedford Creek G.C.

PO Box 70 • Zip 13685

Phone	(315) 646-3400
Hours Open	Daylight hours
Average Green Fees	$7 - $12
Special Rates?	No
Credit Cards	No
Season	May-October
Amenities	Bar
Dress Code	Shirts must be worn at all times, casual wear
Tee Time Required?	No
Golf Packages Available?	No
10% discount available?	No

Validation_____Score_____Date_____

# of Holes	9	Par	36	Carts	$7	Clubs	$2

Watertown Golf Club, Inc.

Thompson Park • Zip 13601

Phone	(315) 782-8192
Hours Open	7am - dusk
Average Green Fees	$10 - $20 wkdays
Special Rates?	Tournaments only
Credit Cards	No
Season	April 1 - November 30
Amenities	Pro shop, lessons, bar, restaurant
Dress Code	No tank tops
Tee Time Required?	Tuesday, Wednesday, Saturday, Sunday
Golf Packages Available?	No
10% discount available?	No

Validation_____Score_____Date_____

# of Holes	Par	Carts	Clubs
18	72	$18	

Willowbrook Golf Club

Rt 37 • Zip 13601

Phone	(315) 782-8192
Hours Open	7 AM - dark
Average Green Fees	$8.50/$13
Special Rates?	No
Credit Cards	No
Season	Weather permitting - October 31
Amenities	Pro Shop, lessons, bar, restaurant
Dress Code	Shirts required at all times
Tee Time Required?	Wkends
Golf Packages Available?	No
10% discount available?	No

Validation_____Score_____Date_____

# of Holes	Par	Carts	Clubs
9/9/9	36/36/36	$9/$16	$5/$8

Brooklyn

Dyker Beach Golf Course

86th & 7th Ave. • Zip 11228

Phone	(718) 836-9722
Hours Open	Daylight hours
Average Green Fees	$10 - $20
Special Rates?	Wkdays & after 4 PM
Credit Cards	MC/VISA
Season	All year
Amenities	Snack bar, $10 deposit for cart rentals
Dress Code	No tank tops
Tee Time Required?	Yes - advanced reservations (718)225-GOLF
Golf Packages Available?	Yes
10% discount available?	No

Validation_____Score_____Date_____

# of Holes	18	Par	71	Carts	$15-$25	Clubs	$25

Brantingham Golf Club
PO Box 151 • Zip 13312

Phone	(315) 348-8861
Hours Open	Daylight hours
Average Green Fees	$10 - $20 Wkdays
Special Rates?	$7 after 5 PM
Credit Cards	No
Season	April 15 - October 15
Amenities	Pro shop, bar, restaurant
Dress Code	No
Tee Time Required?	No
Golf Packages Available?	Yes
10% discount available?	Yes

Validation_____Score_____Date_____

# of Holes	18	Par	71	Carts	$9/$15	Clubs	$2

Cedars Golf Course
East Road • Zip 13367

Phone	(315) 376-6267
Hours Open	Daylight hours
Average Green Fees	$10
Special Rates?	After 6 PM
Credit Cards	No
Season	April 1 - First snowfall
Amenities	Club house, snack bar, full liquor bar
Dress Code	Shirts worn at all times
Tee Time Required?	No
Golf Packages Available?	No
10% discount available?	Inquire

Validation_____Score_____Date_____

# of Holes	18	Par	72	Carts	$8/$14	Clubs	$2

Turin Highlands

East Road • Zip 13473

Phone	(315) 348-9912
Hours Open	Daylight hours
Average Green Fees	$12
Special Rates?	After 5 PM - $7
Credit Cards	No
Season	May 1 - October 15
Amenities	Pro shop, bar, restaurant
Dress Code	Proper golf attire
Tee Time Required?	Recommended
Golf Packages Available?	Towpath Inn guests, mid-week or wkend
10% discount available?	Yes

Validation_____Score_____Date_____

# of Holes	18	Par	72	Carts	YES	Clubs	YES

Avon

Farview Golf & Country Inn
2419 Avon Genesee Rd. • Zip 14414

Phone	(716) 226-8210
Hours Open	Daylight hours
Average Green Fees	$8.50 /$15
Special Rates?	No
Credit Cards	No
Season	March - November
Amenities	Bar, snack bar, pro shop
Dress Code	No
Tee Time Required?	Wkends
Golf Packages Available?	No
10% discount available?	Yes

Validation_____Score_____Date_____

# of Holes	9+	Par	70	Carts	YES	Clubs	YES

Conesus

Whispering Hills G.C.
1 Pine Alley • Zip 14435

Phone	(716)346-2100
Hours Open	Daylight hours
Average Green Fees	$14 wkdays, $15 wkends
Special Rates?	Senior Citizens
Credit Cards	No
Season	April 1 - November
Amenities	Pro shop, lessons with Pierre Meldrum, bar, restaurant, driving range, putting green, short order food service
Dress Code	Collared shirts
Tee Time Required?	Preferred, a must on wkends
Golf Packages Available?	No
10% discount available?	No

Validation_____Score_____Date_____

# of Holes	18	Par	72	Carts	$10/$20	Clubs	YES

Dansville

Brae Burn Golf Course

Red Jacket St. • Zip 14437

Phone	(716) 335-3101
Hours Open	7 AM - dark
Average Green Fees	$8 - $13 wkdays, $10 - $15 wends, holidays
Special Rates?	Senior Citizens
Credit Cards	No
Season	April 1 - November 1
Amenities	Bar, restaurant
Dress Code	Shirts
Tee Time Required?	Sundays
Golf Packages Available?	No
10% discount available?	No

Validation_____Score_____Date_____

# of Holes	9	Par	34	Carts	YES	Clubs	$5

Geneseo

Livingston Country Club

Lakeville Rd. • Zip 14454

Phone	(716) 243-4430
Hours Open	Daylight hours
Average Green Fees	$12 - $14
Special Rates?	No
Credit Cards	MC/VISA
Season	March 15 - November 15
Amenities	Pro shop, lessons, bar, restaurant, driving range, putting green
Dress Code	No tank tops
Tee Time Required?	Yes
Golf Packages Available?	No
10% discount available?	Inquire

Validation_____Score_____Date_____

# of Holes	18	Par	72	Carts	$16	Clubs	NO

Lima

Lima Golf Country Club
2681 Plank Rd. • Zip 14485

Phone	(716) 624-1490
Hours Open	7 AM - dusk wkdays, 5:30 AM - dusk wkends.
Average Green Fees	$15/$16.50
Special Rates?	Senior Citizens
Credit Cards	No
Season	March - November
Amenities	Pro shop, lessons, bar, lunches, driving range
Dress Code	No tank tops
Tee Time Required?	Wkends
Golf Packages Available?	No
10% discount available?	Wkdays only

Validation_____Score_____Date_____

# of Holes	18	Par	72	Carts	YES	Clubs	YES

Nunda

Barberlea Golf Course
Rt. 408 • Zip 14517

Phone	(716) 468-2116
Hours Open	Daylight hours
Average Green Fees	$8 - $12
Special Rates?	Senior Citizens $1 off
Credit Cards	No
Season	April 15 - October 31
Amenities	Pro shop, lessons, snack bar, beer
Dress Code	No
Tee Time Required?	No
Golf Packages Available?	No
10% discount available?	Yes

Validation_____Score_____Date_____

# of Holes	18	Par	69	Carts	$8/$16	Clubs	$2

Sonyea

Keshequa Golf Club

Off Ridge Rd. • Zip 14556

Phone	(716) 658-4545
Hours Open	Daylight hours
Average Green Fees	$8/$10 wkdays, $9/$12 wkends
Special Rates?	No
Credit Cards	No
Season	April 3 - October 30
Amenities	Limited pro shop, snacks
Dress Code	Shirts must be worn at all times
Tee Time Required?	No
Golf Packages Available?	No
10% discount available?	Yes

Validation_____Score_____Date_____

# of Holes	9	Par	34	Carts	PULL	Clubs	YES

Bridgeport

Rogue's Roost Golf Course

Rt. 31 • Zip 13030

Phone	(315) 633-9406
Hours Open	Daylight hours
Average Green Fees	$15
Special Rates?	Wkdays
Credit Cards	No
Season	March - October
Amenities	Pro shop, lessons, bar, restaurant
Dress Code	No
Tee Time Required?	Wkends & holidays
Golf Packages Available?	No
10% discount available?	No

Validation_____Score_____Date_____

# of Holes	18	Par	71	Carts	YES	Clubs	NO

Canastota

Casolwood Golf Club

RR 5 New Boston Rd. • Zip 13032

Phone	(315) 697-9164
Hours Open	7 AM - 10 PM
Average Green Fees	$12
Special Rates?	Senior Citizens
Credit Cards	MC/VISA
Season	St. Patricks Day - December 24
Amenities	Full bar, food, club house, pro shop, banquet service
Dress Code	Shirts, shoes worn at all times
Tee Time Required?	No
Golf Packages Available?	Yes-call for details
10% discount available?	Yes

Validation_____Score_____Date_____

# of Holes	18	Par	71	Carts	$16	Clubs	$3

Chittenango

Skyridge Chalet & Golf
Salt Springs Rd. • Zip 13037

Phone	(315) 687-6900
Hours Open	Daylight hours
Average Green Fees	$6/$8 wkdays, $8/$10 wkends
Special Rates?	Senior Citizens
Credit Cards	
Season	April 1 - November
Amenities	Snack bar, limited pro shop
Dress Code	No
Tee Time Required?	No
Golf Packages Available?	
10% discount available?	Inquire

Validation_____Score_____Date_____

# of Holes	9	Par	35	Carts	$9/$15	Clubs	$6

Oneida

Oneida Country Club
409 Genesee St. • Zip 13421

Phone	(315) 363-8879
Hours Open	Daylight hours
Average Green Fees	$6 wkdays, $7 wkends
Special Rates?	Senior Citizens
Credit Cards	No
Season	April 1 - 1st week in October
Amenities	Complete pro shop, lessons, putting green, driving range under construction
Dress Code	No
Tee Time Required?	No
Golf Packages Available?	No
10% discount available?	No

Validation_____Score_____Date_____

# of Holes	9	Par	29	Carts	$5	Clubs	$6

Bayberry Creek G . C.

7061 Ridge Rd. W. • Zip 14420

Phone	(716) 637-4302
Hours Open	8 AM - 8 PM
Average Green Fees	$10 and under
Special Rates?	
Credit Cards	No
Season	May - October
Amenities	
Dress Code	No
Tee Time Required?	No
Golf Packages Available?	
10% discount available?	Inquire

Validation_____Score_____Date_____

# of Holes	18	Par	68	Carts	YES	Clubs	NO

Brockport Country Club

3739 Monroe Orlns Cty Ln Rd. • Zip 14420

Phone	(716) 638-6486
Hours Open	Daylight hours
Average Green Fees	$12 wkdays, $15 wkends
Special Rates?	Senior Citizens $8 wkdays only
Credit Cards	No
Season	April 1 - November 1 (weather permitting)
Amenities	Pro shop, lessons, bar, restaurant
Dress Code	No
Tee Time Required?	Required wkends
Golf Packages Available?	Yes
10% discount available?	No

Validation_____Score_____Date_____

# of Holes	18	Par	72	Carts	$14/$16	Clubs	YES

Brockport

Deerfield Country Club   100 Craig Hill Dr. • Zip 14420

Phone	(716) 392-8080
Hours Open	6 AM - 7:30 wkdays, sunrise - 7:30 wkends
Average Green Fees	$17/$20
Special Rates?	Senior citizens & juniors before noon
Credit Cards	MC/VISA
Season	April - December 1
Amenities	Restaurant, driving range
Dress Code	No tank tops, cutoffs
Tee Time Required?	Wkdays call ahead (required on wkends)
Golf Packages Available?	No
10% discount available?	Inquire

Validation_____Score_____Date_____

# of Holes	27	Par	72	Carts	$9/$18	Clubs	$4/$8

Fairport

Eagle Vale Golf   4400 Nine Mile Point Rd. • Zip 14450

Phone	(716) 392-5200
Hours Open	6:30 AM - dark
Average Green Fees	$20 - $30
Special Rates?	Senior Citizens before 11 AM wkdays only
Credit Cards	MC/VISA
Season	April 1 - December 1
Amenities	Restaurant, golf learning center indoors and out
Dress Code	Yes
Tee Time Required?	Yes
Golf Packages Available?	No
10% discount available?	Yes

Validation_____Score_____Date_____

# of Holes	18	Par	71	Carts	INCL	Clubs	YES

Fairport

Island Valley Golf

1208 Fairport Rd. • Zip 14450

Phone	(716) 586-1300
Hours Open	Daylight hours
Average Green Fees	$10
Special Rates?	Senior Citizens wkdays only
Credit Cards	No
Season	April 15 - October 31
Amenities	Limited pro shop
Dress Code	Proper golf attire
Tee Time Required?	Preferred
Golf Packages Available?	No
10% discount available?	No

Validation_____Score_____Date_____

# of Holes	9	Par	35	Carts	$8	Clubs	$6

Penfield

Shadow Lake Golf & Racquet

1850 Five Mile Line Rd. • Zip 14526

Phone	(716) 385-1096
Hours Open	Daylight hours
Average Green Fees	$16 - $20
Special Rates?	Senior Citizens
Credit Cards	MC/VISA/AMEX
Season	March - December (weather permitting)
Amenities	Pro shop, restaurant, tennis, beach volleyball, platform tennis, cross-country skiing
Dress Code	No tank tops
Tee Time Required?	Yes
Golf Packages Available?	No
10% discount available?	Inqurie

Validation_____Score_____Date_____

# of Holes	18	Par	71	Carts	YES	Clubs	YES

Penfield

Shadow Pines Golf Club
600 Whalen Rd. • Zip 14526

Phone	(716) 385-8550
Hours Open	Daylight hours
Average Green Fees	$26 - $30
Special Rates?	Senior Citizens
Credit Cards	MC/VISA/AMEX
Season	April - November
Amenities	Golf school, 5 teaching pros, full restaurant
Dress Code	No tank tops
Tee Time Required?	Yes
Golf Packages Available?	No
10% discount available?	Inquire

Validation_____Score_____Date_____

# of Holes	18CHAMP	Par	72	Carts	INCL	Clubs	YES

Penfield

Shadow Pines Golf Club
1850 Five Mile Line Rd. • Zip 14526

Phone	(716) 385-2010
Hours Open	Daylight hours
Average Green Fees	$7 - $10
Special Rates?	Senior Citizens
Credit Cards	MC/VISA/AMEX
Season	March - December (weather permitting)
Amenities	Pro shop, restaurant, racquet club. See also - Shadow Lake Golf & Racquet Club amenities
Dress Code	No tank tops
Tee Time Required?	Bag Line
Golf Packages Available?	No
10% discount available?	No

Validation_____Score_____Date_____

# of Holes	EXEC 9	Par	3's & 4's	Carts	YES	Clubs	YES

Rochester

Genesee Valley G. C.
1000 E. River Rd • Zip 14623.

Phone	(716) 424-2920
Hours Open	7 AM - dusk (Monday - Friday)
	6 AM - dusk (Saturday - Sunday, holidays)
Average Green Fees	
Special Rates?	No
Credit Cards	No
Season	May - November 1
Amenities	Pro shop, lessons, bar, snack bar
Dress Code	No
Tee Time Required?	No
Golf Packages Available?	No
10% discount available?	No

Validation_____Score_____Date_____

# of Holes	2/18	Par	71/67	Carts	YES	Clubs	$5

Rochester

Lake Shore Country Club
1165 Greenleaf Rd. • Zip 14612

Phone	(716) 663-5578
Hours Open	7 AM - dusk
Average Green Fees	$20
Special Rates?	No
Credit Cards	MC/VISA
Season	April - October 31
Amenities	Pro shop, lessons, bar, restaurant, driving range
Dress Code	Collared shirts, no tank tops, cutoffs
Tee Time Required?	Appreciated
Golf Packages Available?	No
10% discount available?	Inquire

Validation_____Score_____Date_____

# of Holes	18	Par	70	Carts	$10	Clubs	NO

Rochester

Latta Lea Par 3

435 Latta Rd. • Zip 14612

Phone	(716) 663-9440
Hours Open	Daylight hours
Average Green Fees	$6
Special Rates?	Senior Citizens
Credit Cards	No
Season	April - November
Amenities	Pro shop, lessons
Dress Code	No
Tee Time Required?	No
Golf Packages Available?	
10% discount available?	No

Validation_____Score_____Date_____

# of Holes	9	Par	27	Carts	YES	Clubs	YES

Rochester

Shore Acres Golf Course

1150 Greenleaf Rd.• Zip 14612

Phone	(716) 621-1030
Hours Open	7 AM - dusk
Average Green Fees	$6
Special Rates?	Call for details
Credit Cards	No
Season	April - October 31
Amenities	Limited pro shop, snack bar
Dress Code	Proper golf attire
Tee Time Required?	No
Golf Packages Available?	No
10% discount available?	No

Validation_____Score_____Date_____

# of Holes	9	Par	Par 3	Carts	NO	Clubs	$3

Rochester

Woodcliff Sports & G.C.

PO Box 22850 • Zip 14692

Phone	(716) 248-4845
Hours Open	6 AM - dusk, Monday - Friday
	7 AM - dusk, Saturday & Sunday
Average Green Fees	$10 and under
Special Rates?	Senior Citizens
Credit Cards	Yes
Season	April - October
Amenities	
Dress Code	Yes
Tee Time Required?	Yes
Golf Packages Available?	Yes
10% discount available?	Inqure

Validation_____Score_____Date_____

# of Holes	9	Par	35	Carts	$5/$10	Clubs	YES

Scottsville

Chili Country Club

760 Scottsville-Chili Rd. • Zip 14546

Phone	(716) 889-9325
Hours Open	7 AM - 9 PM
Average Green Fees	$13/$15
Special Rates?	Call for details
Credit Cards	MC/VISA
Season	Whenever snow is gone
Amenities	Pro shop, lessons, bar, restaurant
Dress Code	No
Tee Time Required?	Wkends
Golf Packages Available?	
10% discount available?	Inquire

Validation_____Score_____Date_____

# of Holes	18	Par	72	Carts	YES	Clubs	$5

Scottsville

Cragie Brae Golf Club

4391 Union St. • Zip 14545

Phone	(716) 889-1440
Hours Open	Daylight hours
Average Green Fees	$10 - $20
Special Rates?	Senior Citizens
Credit Cards	No
Season	April - October
Amenities	Small pro shop, small restaurant
Dress Code	No
Tee Time Required?	No
Golf Packages Available?	No
10% discount available?	Yes

Validation_____Score_____Date_____

# of Holes	18	Par	72	Carts	YES	Clubs	YES

Spencerport

Arrowhead Golf Club

655 Gallup Rd. • Zip 14559

Phone	(716) 352-5500
Hours Open	Daylight hours
Average Green Fees	$7/$14
Special Rates?	Yes
Credit Cards	MC/VISA
Season	Weather permitting
Amenities	Pro shop, snack bar
Dress Code	Proper golf attire
Tee Time Required?	Wkends & holidays
Golf Packages Available?	
10% discount available?	Inquire

Validation_____Score_____Date_____

# of Holes	18	Par	64	Carts	YES	Clubs	YES

Braemar Golf Course

4704 W. Ridge Rd. • Zip 14559

Phone	(716) 352-5360
Hours Open	Daylight hours
Average Green Fees	$9/$13 wkdays, $10/$16 wkends
Special Rates?	Senior Ctizens $8/$10
Credit Cards	No
Season	April 1 - November 30
Amenities	Pro shop, bar, restaurant
Dress Code	No
Tee Time Required?	Wkends
Golf Packages Available?	No
10% discount available?	No

Validation_____Score_____Date_____

# of Holes	18	Par	72	Carts	$10/$18	Clubs	NO

Buttonwood G.C. Par 3

600 Trimmer Rd. • Zip 14559

Phone	(716) 352-4720
Hours Open	Daylight hours
Average Green Fees	$5 - $6 all week
Special Rates?	Children 12 and under
Credit Cards	No
Season	April - November 1
Amenities	Snacks, drinks, putting green, pro shop, option to play 5 extra holes - par 4
Dress Code	Shirts required at all times
Tee Time Required?	No
Golf Packages Available?	No
10% discount available?	No

Validation_____Score_____Date_____

# of Holes	9	Par	27	Carts	YES	Clubs	YES

Spencerport

Twin Hills Golf Course
5719 Ridge Rd. W. • Zip 14559

Phone	(716) 352-4800
Hours Open	Daylight hours
Average Green Fees	$15
Special Rates?	Leagues
Credit Cards	No
Season	April - November
Amenities	Driving range, snack bar
Dress Code	Shirts must be worn at all times
Tee Time Required?	Wkends & holidays in the AM
Golf Packages Available?	No
10% discount available?	No

Validation_____Score_____Date_____

# of Holes	18	Par	71	Carts	YES	Clubs	YES

W. Henrietta

Riverton Golf Club
Scottsville W. Henrietta Rd. • Zip 14586

Phone	(716) 334-6196
Hours Open	Daylight hours
Average Green Fees	$10/$12
Special Rates?	Senior Citizens $5, wkdays only
Credit Cards	MC/VISA
Season	April 1 - October 31
Amenities	Snack bar, driving range, pro shop
Dress Code	Shirts w/collars, shorts just above the knee
Tee Time Required?	Wkends
Golf Packages Available?	No
10% discount available?	Inquire

Validation_____Score_____Date_____

# of Holes	9	Par	36	Carts	$10/$18	Clubs	$5

Webster Golf Course

440 Salt Rd. • Zip 14580

Phone	(716) 265-1920
Hours Open	6 AM - dusk
Average Green Fees	$10 - $20 wkdays
Special Rates?	No
Credit Cards	No
Season	April - November
Amenities	Pro shop, lessons, bar, restaurant, grass tee driving range
Dress Code	Collared shirts, no cutoffs
Tee Time Required?	Yes
Golf Packages Available?	No
10% discount available?	Inquire

Validation_____Score_____Date_____

# of Holes	18/18	Par	70/72	Carts	NO	Clubs	NO

Amsterdam Golf Course

Upper Van Dyke Ave. • Zip 12010

Phone	(518) 842-6480
Hours Open	7 AM - dusk
Average Green Fees	$15
Special Rates?	After 4 PM $10
Credit Cards	No
Season	April - October
Amenities	Pro shop, lessons, bar, restaurant
Dress Code	Shirts required
Tee Time Required?	Wkends
Golf Packages Available?	No
10% discount available?	No

Validation_____Score_____Date_____

# of Holes	18	Par	71	Carts	$16	Clubs	NO

Arthur Carter Muni. G.C.

Van Dyke Ave. • Zip 12010

Phone	(518) 842-1468
Hours Open	Daylight hours
Average Green Fees	$10 /$15 wkdays, $15/$20 wkends
Special Rates?	After 4 PM - $10
Credit Cards	No
Season	April 1 - October 31
Amenities	Clubhouse with full dining facilities, locker rooms, lounge
Dress Code	No
Tee Time Required?	Wkends
Golf Packages Available?	No
10% discount available?	No

Validation_____Score_____Date_____

# of Holes	18	Par	71	Carts	$20	Clubs	$5

Canajoharie Country Club

PO Box 57 • Zip 13317

Phone	(518) 673-8183
Hours Open	Daylight hours
Average Green Fees	$13
Special Rates?	No
Credit Cards	No
Season	April 1 - November 1
Amenities	Pro shop, bar, restaurant
Dress Code	Shirts, casual wear
Tee Time Required?	Wkends
Golf Packages Available?	No
10% discount available?	No

Validation_____Score_____Date_____

# of Holes	18	Par	70	Carts	YES	Clubs	YES

E. Meadow

Eisenhower Park G. C.

Eisenhower Park • Zip 11544

Phone	(516) 542-4528
Hours Open	Daylight hours
Average Green Fees	Cnty. Res. $8/$14, Non.-Res. $20/$30
Special Rates?	Call for details
Credit Cards	No
Season	All year weather permitting
Amenities	Concession stand, driving range, practice & putting greens, snack bars, restaurant, cafeteria, lounge
Dress Code	Shirts, golf shoes must be worn at all times
Tee Time Required?	No, but offered at $4 charge per person
Golf Packages Available?	Honor guest passes from Hotels
10% discount available?	No

Validation_____Score_____Date_____

# of Holes	3/18	Par	72/72	Carts	$20/$30	Clubs	$15

E. Rockaway

Bay Park Golf Course

First Ave. • Zip 11518

Phone	(516) 593-8840
Hours Open	Daylight hours (Closed Wednesday)
Average Green Fees	Re. $7 & $8
Special Rates?	Senior Citizens
Credit Cards	No
Season	March - December
Amenities	Putting area, chipping green, vending machine
Dress Code	No
Tee Time Required?	No
Golf Packages Available?	No
10% discount available?	No

Validation_____Score_____Date_____

# of Holes	9	Par	30	Carts	PULL	Clubs	NO

Farmingdale

Bethpage State Park

Round Swamp Rd. • Zip 11735

Phone	(516) 249-0700
Hours Open	Daylight hours
Average Green Fees	$12/$14 wkdays, $14/$16 wkends & holidays
Special Rates?	After 4 PM
Credit Cards	No
Season	Year round
Amenities	Pro shop, lessons, bar, restaurant
Dress Code	Yes
Tee Time Required?	No
Golf Packages Available?	No
10% discount available?	No

Validation_____Score_____Date_____

# of Holes	5/18	Par	70/72	Carts	YES	Clubs	YES

Glen Cove

Glen Cove Municipal G. C.

Latting Town Rd. • Zip 11542

Phone	(516) 671-0033
Hours Open	Daylight hours
Average Green Fees	Cnty Res. $8 /$12, Non. Res. $9/$11
Special Rates?	Call for details
Credit Cards	No
Season	All year weather permitting
Amenities	Driving range, pro shop, lessons, restaurant, bar, practice putting green
Dress Code	No short shorts, tank tops
Tee Time Required?	No
Golf Packages Available?	With Convention Center
10% discount available?	No

Validation_____Score_____Date_____

# of Holes	18	Par	66	Carts	$19	Clubs	YES

Hicksville

Cantiague Park

West John St. • Zip 11801

Phone	(516) 932-1600
Hours Open	Daylight hours, closed Tuesday
Average Green Fees	Res. $7/$8, Non. Res. $14/$15
Special Rates?	Senior Citizens $3.50 wkdays
Credit Cards	No
Season	All year, weather permitting
Amenities	Pro shop
Dress Code	No
Tee Time Required?	No
Golf Packages Available?	No
10% discount available?	No

Validation_____Score_____Date_____

# of Holes	9	Par	30	Carts	PULL	Clubs	$5

Lido Beach

Lido Golf Club

Lido Blvd. • Zip 11561

Phone	(516) 889-8181, (516) 431-8778 (Pro shop)
Hours Open	7 AM - dusk (Summer hours 6:30AM - dusk) CLOSED TUESDAYS
Average Green Fees	Res. $13.50 Non. Res. $40, Long Bch.Res. $15
Special Rates?	Late rate (3 hours before sundown)
Credit Cards	Pro shop only
Season	All year, weather permitting
Amenities	Pro shop, driving range, putting green at no charge, restaurant, half way house w/light lunches. NO SPECTATORS ALLOWED ON COURSE
Dress Code	Proper golf attire
Tee Time Required?	Call for details
Golf Packages Available?	Call for details
10% discount available?	Inquire

Validation_____Score_____Date_____

# of Holes	18	Par	71	Carts	$21.70	Clubs	$15

Massapequa

Peninsula Golf Club

50 Nassua Rd. • Zip 11758

Phone	(516) 798-9776
Hours Open	Daylight hours
Average Green Fees	$15/$17
Special Rates?	No
Credit Cards	No
Season	All year round
Amenities	Restaurant, putting green, pro shop
Dress Code	No tank tops
Tee Time Required?	No
Golf Packages Available?	No
10% discount available?	Inquire

Validation_____Score_____Date_____

# of Holes	9	Par	37	Carts	YES	Clubs	YES

Merrick

Birdie's & Bogey's Inc.

2550 Clubhouse Rd. • Zip 11566

Phone	(516) 546-7575
Hours Open	Daylight hours, closed Wednesdays
Average Green Fees	$4.50
Special Rates?	Senior Citizens
Credit Cards	Summers only
Season	Year round
Amenities	Restaurant, pro shop, driving range, putting green
Dress Code	No
Tee Time Required?	No
Golf Packages Available?	
10% discount available?	Inquire

Validation_____Score_____Date_____

# of Holes	9	Par	36	Carts	YES	Clubs	YES

Merrick Golf Club
2550 Clubhouse Rd. • Zip 11566

Phone	(516) 868-4650
Hours Open	Daylight hours
Average Green Fees	$7/$9
Special Rates?	Senior Citizens
Credit Cards	No
Season	All year, weather permitting
Amenities	Cafeteria, pro shop
Dress Code	No beach attire
Tee Time Required?	No
Golf Packages Available?	No
10% discount available?	No

Validation_____Score_____Date_____

# of Holes	9	Par	36	Carts	PULL	Clubs	YES

N. Woodmere Golf Course
Branch Blvd. • Zip 11581

Phone	(516) 791-7705
Hours Open	Daylight hours
Average Green Fees	Cnty. Res. w/pass $7/$8, Non. Res. $16/$18
Special Rates?	Senior Citizens
Credit Cards	No
Season	All year, weather permitting
Amenities	Vending machine, pro shop
Dress Code	No
Tee Time Required?	Recoomended
Golf Packages Available?	No
10% discount available?	No

Validation_____Score_____Date_____

# of Holes	9	Par	31	Carts	NO	Clubs	NO

North Hills

Christopher Morley Park
Searing Town Rd. • Zip 11554

Phone	(516) 621-9107
Hours Open	6 AM - 7 PM
Average Green Fees	Cnty.Res. $7/$8, Non.Res. $16/$18
Special Rates?	Call for details
Credit Cards	No
Season	March 15 - December 20
Amenities	Practice putting green
Dress Code	Shirts must be worn at all times
Tee Time Required?	No
Golf Packages Available?	No
10% discount available?	No

Validation_____Score_____Date_____

# of Holes	9	Par	29	Carts	PULL	Clubs	NO

Woodbury

Town of Oyster Bay G.C.
S. Woods Rd. • Zip 11797

Phone	(516) 364-1105
Hours Open	Daylight hours
Average Green Fees	$20/$25
Special Rates?	After 4 PM
Credit Cards	No
Season	April 1 - November 1
Amenities	Driving range, practice putting green, restaurant, lessons
Dress Code	Proper golf attire
Tee Time Required?	No
Golf Packages Available?	No
10% discount available?	No

Validation_____Score_____Date_____

# of Holes	18	Par	70	Carts	$20	Clubs	YES

Niagara County G. C.

314 Davison Rd.• Zip 14094

Phone	(716) 434-6669
Hours Open	Daylight hours
Average Green Fees	$9/$10 NYS Res., $11/$12 Non. Res.
Special Rates?	Call for details
Credit Cards	No
Season	May 1 - October 31
Amenities	Driving range, putting green, restaurant, bar
Dress Code	No
Tee Time Required?	No
Golf Packages Available?	No
10% discount available?	No

Validation_____Score_____Date_____

# of Holes	18	Par	72	Carts	$8/$16	Clubs	YES

Willowbrook Golf Course

4200 Lake Ave. • Zip 14094

Phone	(716) 434-0111
Hours Open	Daylight hours
Average Green Fees	$8/$14 wkdays, $9/$17 wkends
Special Rates?	Senior Citizens
Credit Cards	MC/VISA
Season	
Amenities	Pro shop, lessons, bar, restaurant
Dress Code	Yes
Tee Time Required?	Yes
Golf Packages Available?	Yes
10% discount available?	No

Validation_____Score_____Date_____

# of Holes	18	Par	71	Carts	$16	Clubs	$5

Middleport

Niagara Orleans C.C. | Telegraph Rd. • Zip 14105

Phone	(716) 735-9000
Hours Open	Daylight hours
Average Green Fees	$12 wkdays, $14 wkends
Special Rates?	Senior Citizens $10 wkdays
Credit Cards	No
Season	April 1 - November 30
Amenities	Lounge, bar, snack bar, pro shop
Dress Code	No cutoffs, tank tops
Tee Time Required?	Wkends
Golf Packages Available?	No
10% discount available?	No

Validation_____ Score_____ Date_____

# of Holes	18	Par	71	Carts	$18	Clubs	$5

N. Tonawanda

Deerwood Golf Course | 1818 Sweeney St. • Zip 14120

Phone	(716) 695-8525
Hours Open	Daylight hours
Average Green Fees	City Res. $8/$10.50, Non.Res. $14.50/$17
Special Rates?	City Senior Citizens, juniors only
Credit Cards	No
Season	Mid April - Thanksgiving
Amenities	Pro shop w/golf clinic for residents only, bar, restaurant, driving range, putting green
Dress Code	No
Tee Time Required?	No
Golf Packages Available?	No
10% discount available?	No

Validation_____ Score_____ Date_____

# of Holes	18	Par	71	Carts	$18	Clubs	$5

Niagara Falls

Hyde Park

Porter Rd. • Zip 14302

Phone	(716) 297-2067
Hours Open	Daylight hours
Average Green Fees	$7 - $10/9holes, $13 - $15/18 holes
Special Rates?	60 & over $4.75 for 9 holes
Credit Cards	No
Season	Mid April - Mid November
Amenities	Pro shop, lessons, bar, restaurant, driving range, putting green
Dress Code	Proper golf attire
Tee Time Required?	No
Golf Packages Available?	No
10% discount available?	No

Validation_____Score_____Date_____

# of Holes	18/9/9	**Par**	70/36/35	**Carts**	$9/$17	**Clubs**	$4/$7.50

Niagara Falls

Niagara's Golf Wonderland

2609 Niagara Falls Blvd. • Zip 14304

Phone	(716) 731-5155
Hours Open	8 AM - dark
Average Green Fees	$5/$10
Special Rates?	No
Credit Cards	No
Season	April - November
Amenities	
Dress Code	
Tee Time Required?	No
Golf Packages Available?	No
10% discount available?	No

Validation_____Score_____Date_____

# of Holes	9	**Par**	28	**Carts**	NO	**Clubs**	NO

Sanborn

Shawnee Golf Course
Town Line Rd. • Zip 14132

Phone	(716) 731-5177
Hours Open	Daylight hours
Average Green Fees	$8
Special Rates?	Senior Citizens, Mondays
Credit Cards	No
Season	April - November
Amenities	Pro shop, bar, restaurant, putting green
Dress Code	Shirts & shoes must be worn at all times
Tee Time Required?	No
Golf Packages Available?	Call for details
10% discount available?	Yes

Validation_____Score_____Date_____

# of Holes	9	Par	36	Carts	$8	Clubs	$3.75

Alder Creek

Alder Creek G.C. & C. I.   Rt. 12 PO Box 97 • Zip 13301

Phone	(315) 831-5222 or 831-5388
Hours Open	Daylight hours
Average Green Fees	$10 and under
Special Rates?	Wkdays
Credit Cards	
Season	
Amenities	Pro shop, lessons, bar, restaurant, lodging, golf school
Dress Code	No
Tee Time Required?	No
Golf Packages Available?	Yes
10% discount available?	Yes

Validation_____Score_____Date_____

# of Holes	9	Par	36	Carts	YES	Clubs	

Boonville

Woodgate Pines G. C.   Woodgate Dr. • Zip 13309

Phone	(315) 942-5442
Hours Open	Daylight hours
Average Green Fees	$10/$20
Special Rates?	Wkdays $7/$12
Credit Cards	MC/VISA
Season	April - November
Amenities	Pro shop, lessons, bar, restaurant
Dress Code	Shirts are required
Tee Time Required?	No
Golf Packages Available?	Yes
10% discount available?	No

Validation_____Score_____Date_____

# of Holes	9	Par	36	Carts	YES	Clubs	YES

Durhamville

Brandy Brook Golf Course
Foster Rd. • Zip 13054

Phone	(315) 363-9879
Hours Open	7 AM - dark
Average Green Fees	$8 wkdays, $9 wkends & holidays
Special Rates?	No
Credit Cards	No
Season	April 15 - November 1
Amenities	Snack bar, bar
Dress Code	No
Tee Time Required?	No
Golf Packages Available?	No
10% discount available?	Inquire

Validation_____Score_____Date_____

# of Holes	9	Par	36	Carts	$8/$16	Clubs	NO

New Hartford

Stonebridge G. & C.
Graffenburg Rd. • Zip 13413

Phone	(315) 733-5662
Hours Open	Daylight hours
Average Green Fees	$10/$20
Special Rates?	No
Credit Cards	No
Season	April - October
Amenities	Pro shop, restaurant
Dress Code	No
Tee Time Required?	Appreciated
Golf Packages Available?	No
10% discount available?	Inquire

Validation_____Score_____Date_____

# of Holes	18	Par	72	Carts	YES	Clubs	

New York Mills

Twin Ponds Golf & C. C.
169 Main St. • Zip 13417

Phone	(315) 736-9303
Hours Open	Daylight hours
Average Green Fees	$10/$12
Special Rates?	No
Credit Cards	MC/VISA
Season	April - November
Amenities	Pro shop, bar, restaurant
Dress Code	No
Tee Time Required?	No
Golf Packages Available?	No
10% discount available?	Inquire

Validation_____Score_____Date_____

# of Holes	18	Par	70	Carts	YES	Clubs	YES

Oneida

Pleasant Knolls G.C.
Stony Brook Rd. RR 2 • Zip 13421

Phone	(315) 829-GOLF
Hours Open	Daylight hours
Average Green Fees	$9 wkdys, $10 wkends & holidays
Special Rates?	No
Credit Cards	No
Season	
Amenities	Full liquor license, sandwiches & refreshments, small pro shop, "Best cheeseburgers around!"
Dress Code	Shirts must be worn at all times
Tee Time Required?	No
Golf Packages Available?	No
10% discount available?	No

Validation_____Score_____Date_____

# of Holes	9	Par	36	Carts	$8/$16	Clubs	$4

Oriskany

Oriskany Hills Golf Course

Rt. 69 • Zip 13424

Phone	(315) 736-4540
Hours Open	7 AM - 9 PM
Average Green Fees	$10/$12
Special Rates?	No
Credit Cards	MC/VISA
Season	April - late October
Amenities	Pro shop, lessons, bar, restaurant, practice green
Dress Code	Shirts & shoes must be worn, decent shorts
Tee Time Required?	No
Golf Packages Available?	No
10% discount available?	Inquire

Validation_____Score_____Date_____

# of Holes	9+	Par	35	Carts	YES	Clubs	YES

Oriskany

Shamrock Golf Course

Airport Rd. • Zip 13424

Phone	(315) 336-9858
Hours Open	Daylight hours
Average Green Fees	$9/$11 all day
Special Rates?	After 5:30 PM $6
Credit Cards	All major cards
Season	2nd week in April - October (weather permitting)
Amenities	Pro shop, lessons, bar, restaurant, practice green, driving range nearby
Dress Code	Proper golf attire
Tee Time Required?	No
Golf Packages Available?	No
10% discount available?	No

Validation_____Score_____Date_____

# of Holes	9	Par	35	Carts	$8/$16	Clubs	$4

Barker Brook Golf Course
Rogers Rd. • Zip 13425

Phone	(315) 821-6438
Hours Open	7 AM - dark
Average Green Fees	$12 wkdays, $14 wkends
Special Rates?	No
Credit Cards	MC/VISA
Season	April - November
Amenities	Pro shop, bar, restaurant
Dress Code	Proper golf attire
Tee Time Required?	No
Golf Packages Available?	Yes
10% discount available?	Inquire

Validation_____Score_____Date_____

# of Holes	18	Par	72	Carts	$10/$18	Clubs	$5

Camroden Golf Course
148 Camroden Westernville Rd. • Zip 13440

Phone	(315) 865-5771
Hours Open	Daylight hours
Average Green Fees	$7.50
Special Rates?	No
Credit Cards	No
Season	April - early November
Amenities	Lessons, bar, driving range, putting green
Dress Code	Proper golf attire
Tee Time Required?	No
Golf Packages Available?	No
10% discount available?	Inquire

Validation_____Score_____Date_____

# of Holes	9	Par	36	Carts	$7/$14	Clubs	$5

Delta Knolls Golf Course

8388 Elmer Hill Rd. • Zip 13440

Phone	(315) 337-6173
Hours Open	8 AM - 10 PM
Average Green Fees	Under $10
Special Rates?	
Credit Cards	Pro shop only
Season	Late March - October
Amenities	Pro shop, lessons, driving range, also 18 hole miniature golf, batting cages, sailboard shop
Dress Code	No
Tee Time Required?	No
Golf Packages Available?	
10% discount available?	Inquire

Validation_____Score_____Date_____

# of Holes	9	Par	3	Carts	NO	Clubs	YES

Rome Country Club

RR 6, Box 376 • Zip 13440

Phone	(315) 336-6464
Hours Open	6 AM - 11 PM
Average Green Fees	$15 wkdays, $20 wkends
Special Rates?	Early bird rates
Credit Cards	MC/VISA
Season	Year around
Amenities	Racquetball, sauna, showers, nautilus & free weights, driving range, pro shop
Dress Code	Yes
Tee Time Required?	Yes
Golf Packages Available?	Yes
10% discount available?	No

Validation_____Score_____Date_____

# of Holes	18	Par	72	Carts	$18	Clubs	$5

Rome

Sleepy Hollow Golf Course

Sleepy Hollow Rd. • Zip 13440

Phone	(315) 337-1562
Hours Open	7 AM - dark
Average Green Fees	$12
Special Rates?	Senior Citizens
Credit Cards	No
Season	April 1 - November
Amenities	Pro shop, bar, restaurant, practice green
Dress Code	Proper golf attire
Tee Time Required?	No
Golf Packages Available?	Yes
10% discount available?	Inquire

Validation_____Score_____Date_____

# of Holes	18	Par	68	Carts	$15	Clubs	$5

Sauquoit

Sauquoit Knolls Golf Course

Knolls Dr. • Zip 13456

Phone	(315) 737-8959
Hours Open	Daylight hours
Average Green Fees	$6 - $8/9 holes, $8 - $10/18 holes
Special Rates?	Senior Citizens on Wed. & Fri.
Credit Cards	No
Season	March 15 - November 1
Amenities	Snack bar, bar, pro shop
Dress Code	Shirts required at all times
Tee Time Required?	After 4 PM
Golf Packages Available?	No
10% discount available?	No

Validation_____Score_____Date_____

# of Holes	9	Par	35	Carts	YES	Clubs	YES

Utica

Valley View Golf Course

Valley View Rd. • Zip 13502

Phone	(315) 732-8755
Hours Open	Daylight hours
Average Green Fees	$10 wkdays, $12 wkends
Special Rates?	Senior Citizens
Credit Cards	No
Season	April 1 - October
Amenities	Pro shop, bar, restaurant, putting green, driving range, practice greens
Dress Code	
Tee Time Required?	Recommended
Golf Packages Available?	No
10% discount available?	Inquire

Validation_____Score_____Date_____

# of Holes	18	Par	72	Carts	$17	Clubs	

Westmoreland

Westmoreland Golf Club

Fairway Dr. • Zip 13490

Phone	(315) 853-8914
Hours Open	Daylight hours
Average Green Fees	$8 wkdays, $9 wkends
Special Rates?	No
Credit Cards	No
Season	April - October
Amenities	Bar, kitchen, pro shop
Dress Code	No
Tee Time Required?	No
Golf Packages Available?	No
10% discount available?	Yes

Validation_____Score_____Date_____

# of Holes	9	Par	36	Carts	$8/$16	Clubs	$5

Whitesboro

Domenico's Golf Club
Church Rd. • Zip 13492

Phone	(315) 736-9812
Hours Open	7 AM - dark
Average Green Fees	$10 - $15
Special Rates?	No
Credit Cards	No
Season	April 1 - November 1
Amenities	Restaurant, small pro shop
Dress Code	No tank tops, cutoffs
Tee Time Required?	No
Golf Packages Available?	No
10% discount available?	Inquire

Validation_____Score_____Date_____

# of Holes	18	Par	72	Carts	$17	Clubs	YES

Whitesboro

Hidden Valley Golf Course
Castle Rd. • Zip 13492

Phone	(315) 736-9953
Hours Open	Daylight hours
Average Green Fees	$11 - $13
Special Rates?	No
Credit Cards	No
Season	April - November
Amenities	Pro shop, lessons, bar, restaurant
Dress Code	Shirts
Tee Time Required?	No
Golf Packages Available?	No
10% discount available?	Inquire

Validation_____Score_____Date_____

# of Holes	18	Par	71	Carts	$18	Clubs	YES

Baldwinsville

Foxfire Golf Course

One Village Blvd. • Zip 13027

Phone	(315) 638-2930
Hours Open	Daylight hours
Average Green Fees	$18 wkdays, $20 wkends
Special Rates?	Group rates available
Credit Cards	MC/VISA
Season	March 15 - November 15
Amenities	Pro shop, lessons, bar, restaurant, banquet facilities, 2 tennis courts, driving range
Dress Code	Proper golf attire
Tee Time Required?	Recommended
Golf Packages Available?	Yes
10% discount available?	Yes

Validation_____Score_____Date_____

# of Holes	CHAMP 18	Par	72	Carts	$20	Clubs	$5

Baldwinsville

Ironwood Golf Course

Canton Street Rd. • Zip 13027

Phone	(315) 635-9826
Hours Open	Daylight hours
Average Green Fees	$8
Special Rates?	No
Credit Cards	MC/VISA
Season	Year round-weather permitting
Amenities	Pro shop, bar, restaurant
Dress Code	No
Tee Time Required?	No
Golf Packages Available?	No
10% discount available?	Inquire

Validation_____Score_____Date_____

# of Holes	9	Par	35	Carts	$8/$15	Clubs	YES

Baldwinsville

Radisson Greens G.C.
8055 Potter Rd. • Zip 13027

Phone	(315) 638-0092
Hours Open	Daylight hours
Average Green Fees	$15/$22
Special Rates?	Senior Citizens $18/18 holes
Credit Cards	No
Season	March - November (weather permitting)
Amenities	Restaurant, pro shop, lessons, driving range, putting green
Dress Code	Prohibits jeans & tank tops
Tee Time Required?	Wkends & holidays
Golf Packages Available?	No
10% discount available?	No

Validation_____Score_____Date_____

# of Holes	18	Par		Carts	$10/$20	Clubs	NO

Baldwinsville

Seneca Golf Course
State Fair Blvd. • Zip 13027

Phone	(315) 635-7571
Hours Open	Daylight hours
Average Green Fees	$8/$10 wkdays, $10/$12 wkends
Special Rates?	Senior Citizens
Credit Cards	MC/VISA
Season	March - October
Amenities	Pro shop, lessons, bar, snack shop, driving range, putting green
Dress Code	No
Tee Time Required?	No
Golf Packages Available?	No
10% discount available?	Inquire

Validation_____Score_____Date_____

# of Holes	9	Par	35	Carts	$9/$18	Clubs	$5

Brewertown

Skyline Golf & C.C.
9113 Brewertown Rd. • Zip 13029

Phone	(315) 699-5338
Hours Open	Daylight hours
Average Green Fees	$10 wkdays, $12.50 wkends
Special Rates?	
Credit Cards	No
Season	May - November 1
Amenities	Pro shop,bar, restaurant
Dress Code	
Tee Time Required?	No
Golf Packages Available?	No
10% discount available?	Inquire

Validation_____Score_____Date_____

# of Holes	18	Par	71	Carts	$16	Clubs	YES

Camillus

Camillus Country Club
5690 Bennetts Corners Rd. • Zip 13031

Phone	(315) 672-3770
Hours Open	Daylight hours
Average Green Fees	$14/$17
Special Rates?	Senior Citizens 1/2 price wkdays, wkend. specials
Credit Cards	MC/VISA
Season	April 15 - November
Amenities	Pro shop, lessons, restaurant, bar, practice greens, locker room
Dress Code	No cut offs or tank tops
Tee Time Required?	Wkends only
Golf Packages Available?	No
10% discount available?	Yes

Validation_____Score_____Date_____

# of Holes	18	Par	73	Carts	YES	Clubs	YES

Camillus

Pine Grove Sport Complex
3185 Milton Ave. Ext. • Zip 13031

Phone	(315) 672-9272
Hours Open	Daylight hours
Average Green Fees	$10/$15
Special Rates?	Senior Citizens
Credit Cards	Yes
Season	April 15 - November (weather permitting)
Amenities	Pro shop, bar, restaurant
Dress Code	No
Tee Time Required?	Inquire
Golf Packages Available?	No
10% discount available?	No

Validation_____ Score_____ Date_____

# of Holes	18	Par	71	Carts	YES	Clubs	NO

Camillus

West Hill Golf & Croquet
2500 W. Genesee & Rt. 5

Phone	(315) 672-8677
Hours Open	Daylight hours
Average Green Fees	$12
Special Rates?	
Credit Cards	
Season	April 1 - November 1
Amenities	Pro shop, bar, restaurant
Dress Code	
Tee Time Required?	Yes
Golf Packages Available?	No
10% discount available?	No

Validation_____ Score_____ Date_____

# of Holes	18	Par	54	Carts	$14	Clubs	$3

Camillus

Westvale Golf Club
100 Golf View Dr. • Zip 13031

Phone	(315) 487-9851
Hours Open	Daylight hours
Average Green Fees	$13/$15
Special Rates?	No
Credit Cards	No
Season	April 1 - November (weather permitting)
Amenities	Snack bar, restaurant, banquet facilities, pro shop, lessons, putting green
Dress Code	No
Tee Time Required?	Wkends
Golf Packages Available?	No
10% discount available?	No

Validation_____ Score_____ Date_____

# of Holes	18	Par	67	Carts	$16	Clubs	YES

Cicero

Northern Pines Golf Course
Rt. 31 • Zip 13039

Phone	(315) 699-2939
Hours Open	Daylight hours
Average Green Fees	$8/$12
Special Rates?	Before noon wkdays. 2/cart $20/$28
Credit Cards	MC/VISA
Season	April - October
Amenities	Pro shop, lessons, bar, restaurant
Dress Code	Proper golf attire
Tee Time Required?	No
Golf Packages Available?	Season passes are available
10% discount available?	Inquire

Validation_____ Score_____ Date_____

# of Holes	9	Par	35	Carts	$8/$15	Clubs	$5/$6

Cicero

Wildwood Golf Club
7954 Brewertown Rd. • Zip 13039

Phone	(315) 699-5255
Hours Open	7 AM - dark
Average Green Fees	$7/$10 wkdays, $9/$12 wkends
Special Rates?	Senior Citizens & before 2 PM wkdays
Credit Cards	MC/VISA
Season	May - October
Amenities	Driving range, golf school, snack bar, restaurant, bar, lounge
Dress Code	No
Tee Time Required?	Recommended
Golf Packages Available?	No
10% discount available?	Inquire

Validation_____Score_____Date_____

# of Holes	9/9	Par	3/36	Carts	$9/$15	Clubs	$5

Delphi Falls

Delphi Falls Golf Course
2127 Oran Delphi Rd. • Zip 13051

Phone	(315) 662-3611
Hours Open	Daylight hours
Average Green Fees	$8/$10 wkdays, $10/$12 wkends
Special Rates?	
Credit Cards	
Season	April 15 - Novmber 1
Amenities	Pro shop, food only
Dress Code	Shirts required, no heeled shoes
Tee Time Required?	No
Golf Packages Available?	
10% discount available?	Inquire

Validation_____Score_____Date_____

# of Holes	18	Par	68	Carts	$15/$20	Clubs	YES

E. Syracuse

Arrowhead Golf Course
7185 E. Taft Rd. • Zip 13057

Phone	(315) 656-7563
Hours Open	8 AM - 10 PM
Average Green Fees	$15
Special Rates?	Senior Citizens
Credit Cards	No
Season	April 15 - November 1
Amenities	Pro shop, beer/soda bar, snack shop, chipping/putting green
Dress Code	Shirts must be worn at all times
Tee Time Required?	No
Golf Packages Available?	
10% discount available?	No

Validation_____ Score_____ Date_____

# of Holes	9/18	Par	36/72	Carts	$16	Clubs	$2

E. Syracuse

Wa-Noa Golf Club
6920 Minoa Bridgeport Rd. • Zip 13057

Phone	(315) 656-8213
Hours Open	Daylight hours
Average Green Fees	$14/$15
Special Rates?	
Credit Cards	No
Season	
Amenities	
Dress Code	
Tee Time Required?	Wkends & holidays
Golf Packages Available?	No
10% discount available?	No

Validation_____ Score_____ Date_____

# of Holes	18	Par	70	Carts	$16	Clubs	$4

Fayetteville

Green Lakes State Park

Rt. 5 7000 Green Lakes Rd. • Zip 13066

Phone	(315) 637-6111
Hours Open	Daylight hours
Average Green Fees	$12/$14
Special Rates?	Senior Citizens 1/2 price M-F except holidays
Credit Cards	Pro shop only
Season	April - November (weather permitting)
Amenities	Pro shop w/PGA Class A Pro, concession stand, practice putting green
Dress Code	Proper golf attire
Tee Time Required?	Call (315) 637-GOLF, Thurs .& Fri. 9 AM - noon, wkends & holidays
Golf Packages Available?	No
10% discount available?	No

Validation_____Score_____Date_____

# of Holes	18	Par	71	Carts	$9/$18	Clubs	$5

Fayetteville

Lyndon Golf Course

Fayetteville Rd.• Zip 13066

Phone	(315) 446-1885
Hours Open	Daylight hours
Average Green Fees	$8/$9
Special Rates?	Senior Citizens $6 wkdays
Credit Cards	Pro Shop only
Season	April 1 - November 1 (weather permitting)
Amenities	Pro shop, snack bar
Dress Code	No
Tee Time Required?	No
Golf Packages Available?	No
10% discount available?	No

Validation_____Score_____Date_____

# of Holes	18	Par	65	Carts	PULL	Clubs	NO

Kirkville

Town Isle Golf Course
Town Island Rd. • Zip 13082

Phone	(315) 656-3522
Hours Open	Daylight hours
Average Green Fees	$10
Special Rates?	No
Credit Cards	No
Season	Snow to snow
Amenities	Pro shop, lessons
Dress Code	Knee length shorts must be worn
Tee Time Required?	Wkends
Golf Packages Available?	No
10% discount available?	Inquire

Validation_____Score_____Date_____

# of Holes	18	Par	70	Carts	$17	Clubs	YES

Lafayette

Orchard Valley Golf Course
4693 Cherry Valley Tpk. • Zip 13084

Phone	(315) 677-5180
Hours Open	Daylight hours
Average Green Fees	$8
Special Rates?	Senior Citizens M - F
Credit Cards	MC/VISA
Season	April - November (weather permitting0
Amenities	Pro shop, lessons, bar, restaurant, driving range, putting green
Dress Code	Casual
Tee Time Required?	No
Golf Packages Available?	Yes
10% discount available?	Inquire

Validation_____Score_____Date_____

# of Holes	9	Par	35	Carts	$7	Clubs	$5

Liverpool

Liverpool Golf Course

Morgan Rd. • Zip 13090

Phone	(315) 457-7170
Hours Open	Daylight hours
Average Green Fees	$10/$17
Special Rates?	Senior Citizens
Credit Cards	No
Season	Seasonal, weather permitting
Amenities	Pro shop, lessons, bar, snack bar, putting green, driving range. Only island hole in Central NY
Dress Code	
Tee Time Required?	Wkends
Golf Packages Available?	Tournament golf pkgs
10% discount available?	Inquire

Validation_____Score_____Date_____

# of Holes	18	Par	71	Carts	$12/$18	Clubs	$5

Mattydale

Brooklawn Golf Course

Thompson Rd. • Zip 13211

Phone	(315) 463-1831
Hours Open	Daylight hours
Average Green Fees	$6.50/$11.50
Special Rates?	Yes
Credit Cards	No
Season	Early spring - late fall (weather permitting)
Amenities	Pro shop, snack bar
Dress Code	No
Tee Time Required?	No
Golf Packages Available?	No
10% discount available?	Yes

Validation_____Score_____Date_____

# of Holes	18	Par	64	Carts	$7/$15	Clubs	$6

Skaneateles

Skaneateles Greens G. C.

Bockes Rd. • Zip 13152

Phone	(315) 673-4916
Hours Open	Daylight hours
Average Green Fees	$10/$11 wkdays, $11/$12 wkends
Special Rates?	Senior Citizens
Credit Cards	No
Season	April 1 - October 31
Amenities	Restaurant, bar, pro shop
Dress Code	No
Tee Time Required?	No
Golf Packages Available?	No
10% discount available?	Yes

Validation_____Score_____Date_____

# of Holes	18	Par	70	Carts	$10/$15	Clubs	$5

Syracuse

Drumlins Golf Course

800 Nottingham Rd. • Zip 13214

Phone	(315) 446-5580
Hours Open	6 AM - 9 PM
Average Green Fees	$14
Special Rates?	Senior Citizens
Credit Cards	MC/VISA
Season	April - snowfall
Amenities	Pro shop, lessons, bar, restaurant, driving range
Dress Code	
Tee Time Required?	No
Golf Packages Available?	Call for details
10% discount available?	Yes

Validation_____Score_____Date_____

# of Holes	18	Par	70	Carts	$10.50	Clubs	$5

Syracuse

Pointe East Golf Course
200 Waring Rd. • Zip 13224

Phone	(315) 445-0963
Hours Open	Daylight hours
Average Green Fees	$10
Special Rates?	Call for details
Credit Cards	No
Season	April - November
Amenities	Pro shop
Dress Code	Shirts must be worn at all times
Tee Time Required?	No
Golf Packages Available?	Call for details
10% discount available?	When renting cart

Validation_____Score_____Date_____

# of Holes	9	Par	35	Carts	$15	Clubs	$5

Syracuse

Pope's Grove Golf Course
695 State Fair Blvd. • Zip 13209

Phone	(315) 487-9075
Hours Open	Daylight hours
Average Green Fees	$5.50
Special Rates?	No
Credit Cards	No
Season	April 1 - November 1
Amenities	Bar, carts for Senior Citizens & handicap persons
Dress Code	Yes
Tee Time Required?	No
Golf Packages Available?	No
10% discount available?	No

Validation_____Score_____Date_____

# of Holes	9	Par	29	Carts	LIMITED	Clubs	YES

Syracuse

Tanner Valley Golf Course
4040 Tanner Rd. • Zip 13215

Phone	(315) 492-9856
Hours Open	Daylight hours
Average Green Fees	$14
Special Rates?	After 6 PM - $6
Credit Cards	No
Season	
Amenities	Pro shop, lessons, bar, restaurant
Dress Code	Shirts must be worn at all times
Tee Time Required?	Wkends
Golf Packages Available?	No
10% discount available?	Senior rates on wkdays

Validation_____Score_____Date_____

# of Holes	18	Par	71	Carts	$16	Clubs	$5

Tully

Hill 'n Dale Country Club
Route 80 • Zip 13159

Phone	(315) 696-8362
Hours Open	Daylight hours
Average Green Fees	$9 wkdays, $10 wkends
Special Rates?	No
Credit Cards	No
Season	April 30 - October
Amenities	Restaurant, pro shop
Dress Code	No
Tee Time Required?	No
Golf Packages Available?	No
10% discount available?	Inquire

Validation_____Score_____Date_____

# of Holes	9	Par	35	Carts	$8/$14	Clubs	YES

Tully

Vesper Hills Golf Course
Octagon & Edwards Rd. • Zip 13159

Phone	(315) 696-8328
Hours Open	Daylight hours
Average Green Fees	$7/$9
Special Rates?	Call for details
Credit Cards	No
Season	April -weather permitting
Amenities	Limited pro shop, sandwiches
Dress Code	Shirts required at all times
Tee Time Required?	No
Golf Packages Available?	No
10% discount available?	Yes

Validation_____Score_____Date_____

# of Holes	9	Par	36	Carts	$10	Clubs	$5

Canandaigua

Centerpointe Country Club
1940 Brickyard Rd. • Zip 14425

Phone	(716) 924-5346
Hours Open	Daylight hours
Average Green Fees	$10/$15 wkdays, $12/$18 wkends & holidays
Special Rates?	Senior Citizens $9/$14 wkdays
Credit Cards	MC/VISA
Season	April 1 - November 30
Amenities	Pro shop, restaurant, lounge
Dress Code	No cutoffs or short shorts, collar required
Tee Time Required?	No
Golf Packages Available?	Call for details
10% discount available?	Inquire

Validation_____Score_____Date_____

# of Holes	18	Par	71	Carts	$20	Clubs	YES

Geneva

Big Oak Golf Course
33 Packwood Rd. • Zip 14456

Phone	(315) 789-9419
Hours Open	Daylight hours
Average Green Fees	$15
Special Rates?	Senior Citizens
Credit Cards	Yes
Season	
Amenities	Riding carts, pro shop, lessons, bar, restaurant
Dress Code	Proper golf attire
Tee Time Required?	No
Golf Packages Available?	
10% discount available?	Inquire

Validation_____Score_____Date_____

# of Holes	9	Par	35	Carts	YES	Clubs	YES

Shortsville

Winged Pheasant Golf Links
1433 Sandhill Rd. • Zip 14548

Phone	((716) 289-8846
Hours Open	Daylight hours
Average Green Fees	$10/$15 wkdays, $12/$16 wkends
Special Rates?	Senior Citizens
Credit Cards	MC/VISA
Season	April - November
Amenities	Pro shop, lessons, bar, restaurant
Dress Code	No short shorts or tank tops
Tee Time Required?	Wkends
Golf Packages Available?	Tournaments
10% discount available?	No

Validation_____Score_____Date_____

# of Holes	18	Par	70	Carts	$16	Clubs	YES

Victor

Victor Hills Golf Club
1450 Brace Rd. • Zip 14564

Phone	(716) 924-3480
Hours Open	Daylight hours
Average Green Fees	$7 - $9/9 holes, $12 - $16/18 holes
Special Rates?	No
Credit Cards	MC/VISA
Season	All year (weather permitting)
Amenities	Pro shop, lessons, bar, restaurant
Dress Code	No
Tee Time Required?	Recommended
Golf Packages Available?	No
10% discount available?	No

Validation_____Score_____Date_____

# of Holes	EXEC 9/18	Par	31/72	Carts	$9/9	Clubs	$5

Campbell Hall

Otterkill Country Club
Otter Rd. • Zip 10916

Phone	(914) 427-2301
Hours Open	Daylight hours
Average Green Fees	$30 - open to public on Tues. & Thurs. only
Special Rates?	After 4 PM - $15
Credit Cards	Only for merchandise
Season	April - December
Amenities	
Dress Code	Proper golf attire
Tee Time Required?	No, call on Mondays due to outings
Golf Packages Available?	Group rates
10% discount available?	No

Validation_____Score_____Date_____

# of Holes	18	Par	72	Carts	$10	Clubs	$10

Central Valley

Central Valley Golf Club
210 Smith Clove Rd. • Zip 10917

Phone	(914) 928-6924
Hours Open	Daylight hours
Average Green Fees	$10 and under
Special Rates?	Wkdays & after 4 PM
Credit Cards	
Season	
Amenities	Pro shop, lessons, bar, restaurant
Dress Code	Proper golf attire
Tee Time Required?	Yes
Golf Packages Available?	
10% discount available?	Inquire

Validation_____Score_____Date_____

# of Holes	18	Par	71	Carts	$15	Clubs	$10

Johnson

Green Ridge Golf Club

Gregory Rd.• Zip 10933

Phone	(914) 355-1317
Hours Open	Daylight hours
Average Green Fees	$11 wkedays, $15 wkends
Special Rates?	Wkdays
Credit Cards	No
Season	
Amenities	Rental equipment, food, beverages
Dress Code	No
Tee Time Required?	No
Golf Packages Available?	
10% discount available?	Inquire

Validation_____Score_____Date_____

# of Holes	9	Par	36	Carts	$11/$20	Clubs	$5

Monroe

Monroe Country Club

Still Rd. • Zip 10950

Phone	(914) 783-9045
Hours Open	7 AM - dusk
Average Green Fees	$18
Special Rates?	Senior Citizens
Credit Cards	No
Season	April 15 - October 31
Amenities	
Dress Code	Yes
Tee Time Required?	No
Golf Packages Available?	No
10% discount available?	Inquire

Validation_____Score_____Date_____

# of Holes	9 DOUBLE	Par	70	Carts	$25	Clubs	YES

Montgomery

Scott's Corners Golf Course

1207 Rt. 17K • Zip 12549

Phone	(914) 457-9141
Hours Open	Daylight hours
Average Green Fees	$11 wkdays, $14 wkends
Special Rates?	Senior Citizens $7 before noon wkdays
Credit Cards	MC/VISA
Season	April - 1st snow
Amenities	Snack bar, pro shop
Dress Code	Proper golf attire
Tee Time Required?	No
Golf Packages Available?	No
10% discount available?	Inquire

Validation_____Score_____Date_____

# of Holes	9	Par	72	Carts	$11/$20	Clubs	$8

Montgomery

Stony Ford

Rt. 416 • Zip 12549

Phone	(914) 457-3000
Hours Open	Daylight hours
Average Green Fees	$10 and under
Special Rates?	Wkdays
Credit Cards	No
Season	
Amenities	Riding carts, pro shop, lessons, bar, restaurant
Dress Code	Proper golf attire
Tee Time Required?	Yes
Golf Packages Available?	
10% discount available?	Inquire

Validation_____Score_____Date_____

# of Holes	18	Par	72	Carts	$15	Clubs	$15

New Windsor

Wood Park Par 3W Golf
RD #2 Mt. Airy Rd. PO Box 377 • Zip 12553

Phone	(914) 564-6529
Hours Open	9 AM -dusk
Average Green Fees	$5/9 holes, $8/18 holes
Special Rates?	Senior Citizens, $1 off
Credit Cards	No
Season	April - October
Amenities	Driving range, putting green, picnic area
Dress Code	No
Tee Time Required?	No
Golf Packages Available?	
10% discount available?	Inquire

Validation_____Score_____Date_____

# of Holes	18	Par	3	Carts	NO	Clubs	NO

Newburgh

Newburgh Country Club
Rt. 17K • Zip 12550

Phone	(914) 561-9350
Hours Open	Daylight hours
Average Green Fees	$10 and under
Special Rates?	Wkdays
Credit Cards	
Season	
Amenities	Rental equipment, food, beverages
Dress Code	
Tee Time Required?	
Golf Packages Available?	
10% discount available?	

Validation_____Score_____Date_____

# of Holes	18	Par	71	Carts	$15	Clubs	

Sparrow Bush

Eddy Farm Hotel & Resort Eddy Farm Rd. PO Box 555 • Zip 12780

Phone	(914) 858-4333
Hours Open	Daylight hours-call first, course only open to public when available
Average Green Fees	$12, $4/9 holes par 3
Special Rates?	No
Credit Cards	No
Season	April - October
Amenities	Used only in conjunction w/hotel reservations: pro shop, restaurant, tennis courts, electric carts, shuffleboard, bocce, swimming, fishing
Dress Code	Proper golf attire
Tee Time Required?	No
Golf Packages Available?	Yes - see above
10% discount available?	Inquire

Validation_____Score_____Date_____

# of Holes	9/9	Par		Carts	$18	Clubs	$3

Westtown

Tamaqua Golf Course Fourd Lea Rd. • Zip 10998

Phone	(914) 726-3660
Hours Open	Daylight hours
Average Green Fees	$3/$7
Special Rates?	Senior Citizens
Credit Cards	No
Season	All year (weather permitting)
Amenities	Snack bar
Dress Code	No
Tee Time Required?	No
Golf Packages Available?	No
10% discount available?	Inquire

Validation_____Score_____Date_____

# of Holes	9	Par	27	Carts	NO	Clubs	YES

Warwick

Hickory Hill Golf Course

Mount Peter Rd. • Zip 10990

Phone	(914) 986-7100
Hours Open	Daylight hours
Average Green Fees	Res. $12 - $14, Non. Res. $24 - $28
Special Rates?	Call for details
Credit Cards	No
Season	April - October
Amenities	Pro shop, concession area
Dress Code	Shirts required at all times
Tee Time Required?	Recommended
Golf Packages Available?	Yes
10% discount available?	No

Validation_____Score_____Date_____

# of Holes	18	Par	72	Carts	$20-$24	Clubs	$15/$3.50

Albion

Pap-Pap's Par 3 G.C.
3431 Gaines Basin Rd. • Zip 14411

Phone	(716) 589-4004
Hours Open	Daylight hours
Average Green Fees	$4.50 - $5.50
Special Rates?	Senior Citizens - Tues. & Fri. $3.75 all day
Credit Cards	No
Season	April - December 1
Amenities	Limited pro shop, snack bar, beer & wine
Dress Code	Shirts & shoes required
Tee Time Required?	No
Golf Packages Available?	No
10% discount available?	Yes

Validation_____Score_____Date_____

# of Holes	9	Par	27	Carts	PULL	Clubs	$2

Albion

Ricci Meadows G. C.
1939 Oak Orchd Rd., Rt. 98 Box 67 • Zip 14411

Phone	(716) 682-3280
Hours Open	Daylight hours
Average Green Fees	$7/$10 wkdays, $8/$12 wkends
Special Rates?	Seniors Citizens wkdays til 1 PM, Wed. $6
Credit Cards	MC/VISA
Season	April - mid October
Amenities	Bar only
Dress Code	Shirts required
Tee Time Required?	No
Golf Packages Available?	No
10% discount available?	Inquire

Validation_____Score_____Date_____

# of Holes	18	Par	71	Carts	$10/$20	Clubs	YES

Holley

Fox Hollow Run
15856 Lynch Rd. • Zip 14470

Phone	(716) 638-6125 or (716) 638-5537 Pro shop
Hours Open	Daylight hours
Average Green Fees	$5
Special Rates?	No
Credit Cards	No
Season	June - October
Amenities	Pro shop, snack bar
Dress Code	Shirts must be worn at all times
Tee Time Required?	No
Golf Packages Available?	
10% discount available?	Inquire

Validation_____Score_____Date_____

# of Holes	9	Par	36	Carts	$9	Clubs	$5

Lyndonville

White Birch Golf Course
Route 63 • Zip 14098

Phone	(716) 765-2630
Hours Open	Daylight hours
Average Green Fees	$4/$6
Special Rates?	Senior Citizens
Credit Cards	No
Season	April 15 - October 15
Amenities	Bar, restaurant, pro shop
Dress Code	Casual
Tee Time Required?	1st come, 1st serve
Golf Packages Available?	No
10% discount available?	Yes

Validation_____Score_____Date_____

# of Holes	9	Par	27	Carts	YES	Clubs	YES

Waterport

Harbour Pointe C. C.

Rts. 18 & 98 • Zip 14571

Phone	(716) 682-3922
Hours Open	Daylight hours
Average Green Fees	$6/$11
Special Rates?	Senior Citizens on Mondays
Credit Cards	No
Season	April - November
Amenities	Pro shop, lessons, bar, restaurant
Dress Code	No
Tee Time Required?	Wkends & holidays
Golf Packages Available?	No
10% discount available?	Inquire

Validation_____Score_____Date_____

# of Holes	18	Par	70	Carts	YES	Clubs	YES

Central Square

Riverside Country Club

River Rd., County Rt 37 • Zip 13036

Phone	(315) 676-7714
Hours Open	Daylight hours
Average Green Fees	$6/$7
Special Rates?	No
Credit Cards	No
Season	Mid April - November
Amenities	Pro shop, lessons, food only
Dress Code	No
Tee Time Required?	No
Golf Packages Available?	No
10% discount available?	No

Validation_____Score_____Date_____

# of Holes	18	Par	58	Carts	$10	Clubs	No

Cleveland

North Shore Golf Club

Mapleflats Rd. • Zip 13042

Phone	(315) 675-8101
Hours Open	Sat.- Mon. 7:30 AM-10 PM, Tues.-Fri. 9 AM-10 PM
Average Green Fees	$6 for 18 holes
Special Rates?	No
Credit Cards	No
Season	April - October
Amenities	Pro shop, bar, restaurant, lodge
Dress Code	No
Tee Time Required?	No
Golf Packages Available?	
10% discount available?	Inquire

Validation_____Score_____Date_____

# of Holes	9	Par	35	Carts	$6/$11	Clubs	NO

Fulton

Battle Island State G.C.

W. River Rd. N. • Zip 13069

Phone	(315) 593-3408
Hours Open	Daylight hours
Average Green Fees	$14
Special Rates?	Senior Citizens wkdays., 1/2 price NYS residents
Credit Cards	No
Season	April - November
Amenities	Pro shop, lessons, bar, restaurant
Dress Code	
Tee Time Required?	Wkends & holidays
Golf Packages Available?	No
10% discount available?	No

Validation_____Score_____Date_____

# of Holes	18	Par	72	Carts	YES	Clubs	YES

Oswego

Easy Par Golf Course

County Rd. 20 • Zip 13126

Phone	(315) 343-7906
Hours Open	Daylight hours
Average Green Fees	$6/$7
Special Rates?	Senior Citizens
Credit Cards	No
Season	April - October
Amenities	Pro shop, bar, short order restaurant
Dress Code	Shirts must be worn at all times, casual dress
Tee Time Required?	No
Golf Packages Available?	No
10% discount available?	No

Validation_____Score_____Date_____

# of Holes	9	Par	32	Carts	YES	Clubs	YES

Oswego

Griffins' Greens
Southwest • 13126

Phone	(315) 343-2996
Hours Open	Daylight hours
Average Green Fees	$7/9, $11/18
Special Rates?	Seniors before 1 PM wkdays $4/$6
Credit Cards	No
Season	April - October
Amenities	Limited pro shop, snack bar, beer & wine available
Dress Code	Shirts must be worn at all times
Tee Time Required?	No
Golf Packages Available?	No
10% discount available?	No

Validation_____Score_____Date_____

# of Holes	18	Par	70	Carts	$8	Clubs	$2.50

Palermo

Emerald Crest
Route 3 • Zip 13069

Phone	(315) 593-1016
Hours Open	8 AM - 9:30 PM wkdays, 7 AM - 9:30 PM wkends
Average Green Fees	$6/$9
Special Rates?	
Credit Cards	
Season	April - October
Amenities	Pro shop, bar, restaurant
Dress Code	
Tee Time Required?	
Golf Packages Available?	
10% discount available?	Inquire

Validation_____Score_____Date_____

# of Holes	9	Par	35	Carts	YES	Clubs	

Pulaski

Pines Golf Course

6916 Scenic Hwy. Rt. 3 • Zip 13142

Phone	(315) 298-9970
Hours Open	8 AM - 9 PM wkdays, 7 AM - 8 PM wkends
Average Green Fees	$5/$8
Special Rates?	
Credit Cards	
Season	April - October
Amenities	Pro shop, bar only
Dress Code	
Tee Time Required?	No
Golf Packages Available?	
10% discount available?	Inquire

Validation_____Score_____Date_____

# of Holes	9	Par	36	Carts	YES	Clubs	

Sandy Creek

Elms Golf Club

9613 Elms Rd. N. • Zip 13145

Phone	(315) 387-5297
Hours Open	Daylight hours
Average Green Fees	$13 wkdays, $15 wkends
Special Rates?	No
Credit Cards	MC/VISA
Season	April - October
Amenities	Pro shop, lessons, bar, restaurant
Dress Code	Proper golf attire
Tee Time Required?	Wkends
Golf Packages Available?	No
10% discount available?	Yes

Validation_____Score_____Date_____

# of Holes	18	Par	70	Carts	$18	Clubs	$3

West Monroe

Greenview Golf Course
Whig Hill Rd. Rt. 49 • Zip 13167

Phone	(315) 668-2244
Hours Open	Daylight hours
Average Green Fees	$9 wkdays, $15 wkends
Special Rates?	No
Credit Cards	No
Season	Mid April - November 1
Amenities	Bar, restaurant
Dress Code	No
Tee Time Required?	No
Golf Packages Available?	Specials during the week
10% discount available?	No

Validation_____Score_____Date_____

# of Holes	36	Par	72	Carts	YES	Clubs	YES

Leatherstocking G.C.

Nelson Ave. • Zip 13326

Phone	(607) 547-5275
Hours Open	Daylight hours
Average Green Fees	$35 wkdays, $45 wkends
Special Rates?	No
Credit Cards	MC/VISA/AMEX
Season	April 25 - November 1
Amenities	Restaurant, pro shop, putting green, 150 room hotel, all new Titleist golf clubs for rent
Dress Code	No jeans, tank tops, halters, proper golf attire
Tee Time Required?	Yes
Golf Packages Available?	Yes
10% discount available?	Inquire

Validation_____Score_____Date_____

# of Holes	18	Par	72	Carts	$24	Clubs	$20

Cee Jay Golf Course

RR1 Box 127 Bateman Rd. • Zip 13796

Phone	(617) 263-5291
Hours Open	Daylight hours
Average Green Fees	$5/$10
Special Rates?	Senior Citizens
Credit Cards	No
Season	April - October 31
Amenities	Limited pro shop, snack bar
Dress Code	Shirts must be worn at all time
Tee Time Required?	No
Golf Packages Available?	No
10% discount available?	Yes

Validation_____Score_____Date_____

# of Holes	18	Par	69	Carts	YES	Clubs	YES

Laurens

Edgewood Golf Course
RR 1, Box 166 • Zip 13796

Phone	(607) 432-9789
Hours Open	7 AM - dusk
Average Green Fees	$7
Special Rates?	Senior Citizens
Credit Cards	No
Season	April 15 - October 15
Amenities	Pro shop, food only, double tees
Dress Code	
Tee Time Required?	No
Golf Packages Available?	No
10% discount available?	No

Validation_____Score_____Date_____

# of Holes	9	Par	72	Carts	$13/18	Clubs	$7

Leonardsville

Summit Lake Golf Course
County Rt. 19

Phone	(315) 855-4389
Hours Open	Daylight hours
Average Green Fees	$7/$8 wkdays
Special Rates?	Senior Citizens
Credit Cards	No
Season	April - November
Amenities	Snack bar, newly refurbished-just opening
Dress Code	Shirts required at all times
Tee Time Required?	No
Golf Packages Available?	No
10% discount available?	Yes

Validation_____Score_____Date_____

# of Holes	9	Par		Carts	$8/$14	Clubs	

Springfield Center

Otsego Golf Club	PO Box 217 • Zip 13468

Phone	(607) 547-9290
Hours Open	8 AM - 7 PM wkdays, 7 AM - 7 PM wkends
Average Green Fees	$15
Special Rates?	Call for details
Credit Cards	No
Season	Late April - late October
Amenities	Food only
Dress Code	Shirts & shoes required
Tee Time Required?	No
Golf Packages Available?	No
10% discount available?	No

Validation_____Score_____Date_____

# of Holes	9	Par	35	Carts	$10/9	Clubs	$10

W. Oneonta

Woodhaven Park G.C.	Forest Lane • Zip 13861

Phone	(607) 433-2301
Hours Open	Daylight hours
Average Green Fees	$10
Special Rates?	Senior Citizens
Credit Cards	No
Season	April - October 31
Amenities	Driving range, pro shop, snack bar, restaurant
Dress Code	No
Tee Time Required?	No
Golf Packages Available?	No
10% discount available?	Yes

Validation_____Score_____Date_____

# of Holes	9	Par	34	Carts	YES	Clubs	YES

Brewster

Vails Grove Golf Course

Peach Lk. RR 2 • Zip 10509

Phone	(914) 669-5721
Hours Open	Daylight hours, open to public M-F, Saturday & Sunday after 2 PM
Average Green Fees	$15
Special Rates?	After 6 PM $8
Credit Cards	No
Season	April - November 30
Amenities	Snacks, beer & soda, limited pro shop
Dress Code	No tank tops
Tee Time Required?	No
Golf Packages Available?	No
10% discount available?	No

Validation_____Score_____Date_____

# of Holes	9	Par	33	Carts	$10/$18	Clubs	NO

Garrison

Garrison Golf Club

Rt. 9 • Zip 10524

Phone	(914) 424-3604
Hours Open	Daylight hours
Average Green Fees	$25 wkdays, $40 wkends
Special Rates?	Wkdays
Credit Cards	Yes
Season	April - November
Amenities	Pro shop, lessons, bar, restaurant
Dress Code	Collared shirts
Tee Time Required?	No
Golf Packages Available?	No
10% discount available?	No

Validation_____Score_____Date_____

# of Holes	18	Par	71	Carts	YES	Clubs	YES

Mahopac

Putnam Country Club

Hill Street • Zip 10541

Phone	(914) 628-3451
Hours Open	Daylight hours
Average Green Fees	$10/$20
Special Rates?	Wkdays & after 4 PM
Credit Cards	No
Season	April - November
Amenities	Pro shop, lessons, food only
Dress Code	Yes
Tee Time Required?	Yes
Golf Packages Available?	No
10% discount available?	No

Validation_____Score_____Date_____

# of Holes	18	Par	71	Carts	$10/$15	Clubs	YES

Flushing

Clearview Golf Courses   202-12 Willets Point Blvd.

Phone	(718) 229-2570
Hours Open	Daylight hours
Average Green Fees	$14/$16
Special Rates?	Twilight, Senior Citizens & Juniors
Credit Cards	MC/VISA
Season	March - October
Amenities	Pro shop, snack bar
Dress Code	No
Tee Time Required?	Appreciated
Golf Packages Available?	No
10% discount available?	Inquire

Validation_____Score_____Date_____

# of Holes	18	Par	70	Carts	YES	Clubs	YES

Flushing

Kissena Park Golf Course   16415 Booth Memorial Ave. • Zip 11365

Phone	(718) 939-4594
Hours Open	Daylight hours
Average Green Fees	$14
Special Rates?	Senior Citizens w/permit
Credit Cards	No
Season	Year long weather permitting
Amenities	
Dress Code	No
Tee Time Required?	Recommend in spring & summer
Golf Packages Available?	No
10% discount available?	No

Validation_____Score_____Date_____

# of Holes	18	Par	64	Carts	YES	Clubs	YES

Woodhaven

Forest Park Golf Course
Park Lane S. & Forest Parkway • Zip 11421

Phone	(718) 296-0999
Hours Open	Daylight hours
Average Green Fees	$14 wkdays, $16 wkends & holidays
Special Rates?	Senior Citizens
Credit Cards	No
Season	April 1 - November 1
Amenities	Food concession
Dress Code	Appropriate golf attire
Tee Time Required?	Yes
Golf Packages Available?	No
10% discount available?	Inquire

Validation_____Score_____Date_____

# of Holes	18	Par	67	Carts	$20	Clubs	$10

Burden Lake C.C.
RD 3 Box 179A Totem Lodge Rd. • Zip 12018

Phone	(518) 674-8917
Hours Open	7 AM - 6 PM
Average Green Fees	$9/$13 wkdays, $11/$16 wkends
Special Rates?	No
Credit Cards	MC/VISA/AMEX/DISC
Season	April - December
Amenities	Restaurant, bar, driving range, putting green, pro shop, banquet facilities
Dress Code	No
Tee Time Required?	Yes
Golf Packages Available? **10% discount available?**	Inquire

Validation_____Score_____Date_____

# of Holes	9	Par	36	Carts	$9/9	Clubs	$5

Evergreen Golf Course
1400 Schuurman Rd. • Zip 12033

Phone	(518) 477-7921
Hours Open	7 AM - dusk
Average Green Fees	$14
Special Rates?	Senior Citizens
Credit Cards	No
Season	All year, weather permitting
Amenities	Pro shop, lessons, bar, restaurant, banquet house
Dress Code	No cutoff shorts or tank tops
Tee Time Required?	No
Golf Packages Available?	No
10% discount available?	Inquire

Validation_____Score_____Date_____

# of Holes	18/18	Par	70/72	Carts	$20	Clubs	$10

Castleton on Hudson

Pheasant Hollow G.C.
2670 Phillips Rd. • Zip 12033

Phone	(518) 477-7921
Hours Open	7 AM - dusk
Average Green Fees	$9
Special Rates?	Senior Citizens
Credit Cards	No
Season	Mid March - October
Amenities	
Dress Code	No cutoff shorts or tank tops
Tee Time Required?	No
Golf Packages Available?	No
10% discount available?	Inquire

Validation_____Score_____Date_____

# of Holes	9	Par	39	Carts	$10	Clubs	

Hoosick Falls

Hoosick Falls Golf Course
Richmond Ave. • Zip 12090

Phone	(518) 686-4210
Hours Open	7 AM - dusk
Average Green Fees	$10/$15
Special Rates?	No
Credit Cards	No
Season	April - November
Amenities	Pro shop, lessons, bar, restaurant, putting green, locker room
Dress Code	Shirt and shoes required
Tee Time Required?	No
Golf Packages Available?	No
10% discount available?	Yes

Validation_____Score_____Date_____

# of Holes	9	Par	34	Carts	$10/$15	Clubs	NO

Troy

Frear Park Golf Course

Oakwood Ave. & Frear Park Blvd. • Zip 12180

Phone	(518) 270-4600
Hours Open	7 AM -dusk
Average Green Fees	$11 wkdays, $13 wkends
Special Rates?	Call for details
Credit Cards	No
Season	April - November
Amenities	Pro shop, lessons, bar, restaurant
Dress Code	Shirts must be worn at all times
Tee Time Required?	Wkends only
Golf Packages Available?	No
10% discount available?	Inquire

Validation_____Score_____Date_____

# of Holes		Par		Carts		Clubs	
	18		71		$9/$17		$5

Staten Island

La Tourette Golf Course

1001 Richmond Hill Rd. • Zip 10306

Phone	(718) 351-1889
Hours Open	Daylight hours
Average Green Fees	$10/$20
Special Rates?	Senior Citizens, Juniors & Twilight
Credit Cards	MC/VISA
Season	March - November
Amenities	
Dress Code	No tank tops or short shorts
Tee Time Required?	Recommended
Golf Packages Available?	
10% discount available?	Inquire

Validation_____Score_____Date_____

# of Holes	18	Par	72	Carts	YES	Clubs	YES

Staten Island

Silver Lake Golf Course

915 Victory Blvd. • Zip 10301

Phone	(718) 447-5686
Hours Open	Sunrise - sunset
Average Green Fees	$14 wkdays, $16 wkends
Special Rates?	Call for details
Credit Cards	MC/VISA
Season	All year
Amenities	Restaurant, putting green
Dress Code	No short shorts or tank tops
Tee Time Required?	Summertime & wkends required
Golf Packages Available?	
10% discount available?	Inquire

Validation_____Score_____Date_____

# of Holes	18	Par	69	Carts	$21.50	Clubs	$13.50

Congers

Rockland Lakes State Park

Rt. 9 W • Zip 10920

Phone	(914) 268-7275
Hours Open	Daylight hours
Average Green Fees	$10 and under
Special Rates?	Wkdays
Credit Cards	No
Season	
Amenities	Pro shop, lessons, food
Dress Code	No
Tee Time Required?	Wkends
Golf Packages Available?	
10% discount available?	Inquire

Validation_____Score_____Date_____

# of Holes	18	Par	72	Carts	$15	Clubs	YES

Pearl River

Blue Hill Golf Club

285 Blue Hill Rd. • Zip 10965

Phone	(914) 735-2094
Hours Open	Daylight hours
Average Green Fees	$10 and under
Special Rates?	Wkdays
Credit Cards	No
Season	
Amenities	Pro shop, lessons, bar & restaurant
Dress Code	No cutoffs or tee shirts
Tee Time Required?	Yes
Golf Packages Available?	
10% discount available?	Inquire

Validation_____Score_____Date_____

# of Holes	18	Par	72	Carts	$15	Clubs	

Suffern

Ramapo Spook Rock G.C.
199 Spook Rock Rd. • Zip 10901

Phone	(914) 357-6466
Hours Open	Daylight hours
Average Green Fees	$10 and under
Special Rates?	Wkdays
Credit Cards	No
Season	
Amenities	Pro shop
Dress Code	No
Tee Time Required?	Yes
Golf Packages Available?	
10% discount available?	Inquire

Validation_____Score_____Date_____

# of Holes	18	Par	72	Carts	$15	Clubs	

Thiells

Town of Haverstraw G.C.
Thiells-Mount Ivy Rd. • Zip 10984

Phone	(914) 354-1616
Hours Open	Daylight hours
Average Green Fees	$19 wkdays, $26 wkends
Special Rates?	Group rates available
Credit Cards	No
Season	March 1 - December 31 (weather permitting)
Amenities	Restaurant
Dress Code	No tank tops or short shorts
Tee Time Required?	Wkends
Golf Packages Available?	No
10% discount available?	No

Validation_____Score_____Date_____

# of Holes	18	Par	72	Carts	$19	Clubs	$10

Ballston Lake

Eagle Crest Golf Club
1004 Ballston Lake Rd Rt. 146A • Zip 12019.

Phone	(518) 877-7082
Hours Open	Daylight hours
Average Green Fees	$15 wkdays, $18 wkends
Special Rates?	Senior Citizens-wkdays
Credit Cards	No
Season	March 20 - November 30
Amenities	Pro shop, bar, restaurant, driving range
Dress Code	No tank tops or cutoffs
Tee Time Required?	Wkends only
Golf Packages Available?	Yes
10% discount available?	Inquire

Validation_____Score_____Date_____

# of Holes	18	Par	72	Carts	$20	Clubs	$8

Galway

Galway Golf Course
5817 Jockey St. • Zip 12074

Phone	(518) 882-6395
Hours Open	Daylight hours
Average Green Fees	$10 and under
Special Rates?	Yes
Credit Cards	No
Season	April - October
Amenities	
Dress Code	No
Tee Time Required?	No
Golf Packages Available?	No
10% discount available?	Inquire

Validation_____Score_____Date_____

# of Holes	EXEC 9	Par	28	Carts	PULL	Clubs	YES

Greenfield Center

Brookhaven Golf Course
Alpine Meadows Rd. • Zip 12833

Phone	(518) 893-7458
Hours Open	Daylight hours
Average Green Fees	$10 and under
Special Rates?	No
Credit Cards	No
Season	
Amenities	Pro shop, bar, restaurant
Dress Code	No tank tops
Tee Time Required?	Wkends
Golf Packages Available?	
10% discount available?	Inquire

Validation_____Score_____Date_____

# of Holes	18	Par	71	Carts	$18	Clubs	$10

Hadley

Bend of the River G.C.
Rt. 9 N • Zip 12835

Phone	(518) 696-3415
Hours Open	Daylight hours
Average Green Fees	$10 and under
Special Rates?	Senior Citizens on Wed.
Credit Cards	No
Season	
Amenities	Pro shop, lessons, bar, restaurant
Dress Code	No
Tee Time Required?	No
Golf Packages Available?	
10% discount available?	Inquire

Validation_____Score_____Date_____

# of Holes	9	Par	35	Carts	$9	Clubs	$5

Jonesville

Van Patten Golf Course

Main St. • Zip 12098

Phone	(518) 877-5400
Hours Open	Daylight hours
Average Green Fees	$10/$20
Special Rates?	Senior Citizens
Credit Cards	No
Season	
Amenities	Pro shop, bar, restaurant
Dress Code	No tank tops
Tee Time Required?	No
Golf Packages Available?	
10% discount available?	Inquire

Validation_____Score_____Date_____

# of Holes	9/9/9	Par	37/36/36	Carts	$18	Clubs	$5/$10

Mechanicville

Mechanicville G.C.

PO Box 462 • Zip 12118

Phone	(518) 664-3866
Hours Open	Daylight hours
Average Green Fees	$12/$18
Special Rates?	Call for details
Credit Cards	No
Season	
Amenities	Pro shop, lessons, bar, restaurant
Dress Code	Collared shirts must be worn at all times, no cutoffs
Tee Time Required?	Saturdays
Golf Packages Available?	
10% discount available?	Inquire

Validation_____Score_____Date_____

# of Holes	9	Par	72	Carts	YES	Clubs	YES

Rexford

Riverview Golf Course

Riverview Rd. • Zip 12148

Phone	(518) 399-1920
Hours Open	Daylight hours
Average Green Fees	$10/$10
Special Rates?	
Credit Cards	
Season	
Amenities	Pro shop, lessons, bar, restaurant
Dress Code	
Tee Time Required?	
Golf Packages Available?	
10% discount available?	Inquire

Validation_____Score_____Date_____

# of Holes	18	Par	73	Carts		Clubs	

S. Glens Falls

Tee-Bird Country Club

Resevoir Rd. • Zip 12803

Phone	(518) 792-7727
Hours Open	Daylight hours
Average Green Fees	$14
Special Rates?	After 5 PM
Credit Cards	On merchandise only
Season	April - November
Amenities	Driving range, pro shop, snacks
Dress Code	Shirts must be worn at all times
Tee Time Required?	Wkends & holidays
Golf Packages Available?	No
10% discount available?	No

Validation_____Score_____Date_____

# of Holes	18	Par	70	Carts	YES	Clubs	YES

Saratoga Springs

J. Victor Skiff

Saratoga Spa State Park • Zip 12866

Phone	(518) 584-2007
Hours Open	Daylight hours
Average Green Fees	$9 wkdays, $11 wkends & holidays
Special Rates?	Senior Citizens $5
Credit Cards	No
Season	Mid April - mid November
Amenities	
Dress Code	No
Tee Time Required?	No
Golf Packages Available?	No
10% discount available?	No

Validation_____ Score_____ Date_____

# of Holes	9	Par	29	Carts	YES	Clubs	YES

Saratoga Springs

Saratoga Spa Championship State Pk

Zip 12866

Phone	(518) 584-2008
Hours Open	Daylight hours
Average Green Fees	$12 wkdays, $14 wkends & holidays
Special Rates?	Senior Citizens $6 wkdays
Credit Cards	No
Season	Mid April - mid November
Amenities	Pro shop, lessons, bar, restaurant
Dress Code	No
Tee Time Required?	No
Golf Packages Available?	No
10% discount available?	No

Validation_____ Score_____ Date_____

# of Holes	18	Par	72	Carts	YES	Clubs	YES

Duanesburg

Hillcrest Golf Club

Giffords Church Rd. • Zip 12056

Phone	(518) 355-9817
Hours Open	Daylight hours
Average Green Fees	Undetermined
Special Rates?	
Credit Cards	No
Season	April - October
Amenities	Pro shop, bar, snack bar
Dress Code	Shirts must be worn at all times
Tee Time Required?	No
Golf Packages Available?	No
10% discount available?	Inquire

Validation_____Score_____Date_____

# of Holes	9	Par	36	Carts	$1/hole	Clubs	NO

Schenectady

Colonie Golf Course

418 Consaul Rd. • Zip 12304

Phone	(518) 374-4181
Hours Open	Daylight hours
Average Green Fees	Res. $11/$13, Non-Res. $18/$19
Special Rates?	Senior Citizens
Credit Cards	No
Season	April - November
Amenities	Restaurant, pro shop, lessons, practice putting & driving range, under 14 accompanied by adult, non-resident accompanied by resident
Dress Code	Shts must worn at all times
Tee Time Required?	Yes-48 hours in advance
Golf Packages Available?	No
10% discount available?	Inquire

Validation_____Score_____Date_____

# of Holes	27	Par		Carts	YES	Clubs	NO

Schenectady Golf Course

Golf Rd. • Zip 12304

Phone	(518) 382-5155
Hours Open	Daylight hours
Average Green Fees	$10/$20
Special Rates?	No
Credit Cards	Yes
Season	Mid March - mid December
Amenities	Pro shop, lessons, bar & restaurant
Dress Code	Yes
Tee Time Required?	Yes
Golf Packages Available?	No
10% discount available?	No

Validation_____Score_____Date_____

# of Holes	18	Par	72	Carts	YES	Clubs	YES

Stadium Golf Course

333 Jackson Ave. • Zip 12304

Phone	(518) 374-9104
Hours Open	Daylight hours
Average Green Fees	$10/$20
Special Rates?	Call for details
Credit Cards	MC/VISA
Season	
Amenities	Pro shop, lessons, bar & restaurant
Dress Code	No tank tops or short shorts
Tee Time Required?	Yes, 2 days in advance
Golf Packages Available?	
10% discount available?	Inquire

Validation_____Score_____Date_____

# of Holes	18	Par	71	Carts	YES	Clubs	$6/$10

Schenectady

Sycamore Green Public Golf

Pangburn Rd. • Zip 12306

Phone	(518) 355-6145
Hours Open	Daylight hours
Average Green Fees	$10/$20
Special Rates?	Senior Citizens
Credit Cards	No
Season	April - November
Amenities	Pro shop, restaurant
Dress Code	No
Tee Time Required?	Wkends
Golf Packages Available?	No
10% discount available?	Inquire

Validation_____Score_____Date_____

# of Holes	18	Par	70	Carts	YES	Clubs	NO

Schenectady

Whispering Pines Executive

2208 Helderberg AVe. • Zip 12306

Phone	(518) 355-2724
Hours Open	Daylight hours
Average Green Fees	$10 and under
Special Rates?	
Credit Cards	
Season	
Amenities	Pro shop, lessons, bar & restaurant
Dress Code	
Tee Time Required?	
Golf Packages Available?	
10% discount available?	Inquire

Validation_____Score_____Date_____

# of Holes	9	Par	37	Carts		Clubs	

Cobleskill

Cobleskill Golf & C. C.

Barnerville Rd. Rt. 7 • Zip 12043

Phone	(518) 234-7887
Hours Open	Daylight hours
Average Green Fees	$15 - $20
Special Rates?	After 5 PM
Credit Cards	MC/VISA for pro shop
Season	April - October
Amenities	Pro shop, lessons, bar & restaurant
Dress Code	Proper golf attire
Tee Time Required?	No
Golf Packages Available?	No
10% discount available?	Inquire

Validation_____Score_____Date_____

# of Holes	9	Par	36	Carts	$10 - $20	Clubs	YES

Watkins Glen Golf Club

Seneca Lake Rd. • Zip 14891

Phone	(607) 535-2340
Hours Open	8 AM - 9 PM wkdays, 7 AM - 9 PM wkends
Average Green Fees	9 & 18 hole rates
Special Rates?	Call for details
Credit Cards	No
Season	April 1 - October 31
Amenities	Pro shop, bar & restaurant
Dress Code	Proper golf attire, no tank tops or cutoffs
Tee Time Required?	Wkends
Golf Packages Available?	
10% discount available?	Yes (on green fees)

Validation_____Score_____Date_____

# of Holes	9	Par	36	Carts	$9/$18	Clubs	$5/$10

Seneca Falls

Cayuga Links

2360 State Rt. 89 • Zip 13148

Phone	(315) 568-6597
Hours Open	7 AM - dark
Average Green Fees	$5/$8
Special Rates?	For NYCC students, staff, athletic members
Credit Cards	MC/VISA
Season	April - October 31
Amenities	Pro shop, snack bar
Dress Code	No
Tee Time Required?	No
Golf Packages Available?	No
10% discount available?	Yes

Validation_____Score_____Date_____

# of Holes	EXEC 9	Par	29	Carts	$5/$8	Clubs	YES

Waterloo

Silver Creek Golf Course

1790 E. River Rd. • Zip 13165

Phone	(315) 539-8688
Hours Open	Daylight hours
Average Green Fees	$8/$13 wkdays, $10/$15 wkends
Special Rates?	Senior Citizens
Credit Cards	MC/VISA/AMEX/DISC
Season	April 1 - November 1
Amenities	Driving range, with natural turf, restaurant & bar, practice green, PGA slope rating
Dress Code	Shirts & shoes must be worn at all times
Tee Time Required?	Recommended
Golf Packages Available?	7 AM-3 PM wkdays-$30/18 w/cart for 2 (June-Sept)
10% discount available?	Inquire

Validation_____Score_____Date_____

# of Holes	18	Par	70	Carts	$17	Clubs	$8

Canton

St. Lawrence Golf Course

Potsdam Rd. Rt. 11 • Zip 13617

Phone	(315) 386-4600
Hours Open	Daylight hours
Average Green Fees	$17/$20
Special Rates?	No
Credit Cards	MC/VISA
Season	April 15 - October 15
Amenities	Pro shop, lessons, bar, restaurant
Dress Code	No tank tops
Tee Time Required?	Yes
Golf Packages Available?	Thru Best Western St. Lawrence Univ. Inn
10% discount available?	Inquire

Validation_____Score_____Date_____

# of Holes	18	Par	72	Carts	$18	Clubs	$6

Gouverneur

Fore by Four Golf Course

RR 4 • Zip 13642

Phone	(315) 287-3711
Hours Open	7 AM - ?
Average Green Fees	$9
Special Rates?	Call for details
Credit Cards	No
Season	6 months
Amenities	Pro shop, lessons, bar, restaurant
Dress Code	Normal
Tee Time Required?	Wkends
Golf Packages Available?	No
10% discount available?	No

Validation_____Score_____Date_____

# of Holes	9	Par	35	Carts	$17	Clubs	$5

Massena

Raymondville Golf & Country

Rt. 56 •Zip 13662

Phone	(315) 769-2759
Hours Open	7 AM - 8 PM
Average Green Fees	$17.50
Special Rates?	Senior Citizens
Credit Cards	No
Season	April 10 - October 20
Amenities	Bar, restaurant
Dress Code	Yes
Tee Time Required?	No
Golf Packages Available?	No
10% discount available?	Inquire

Validation_____Score_____Date_____

# of Holes	18	Par	71	Carts	YES	Clubs	YES

Ogdensburg

St. Lawrence State Pk

Riverside Dr. • Zip 13669

Phone	(315) 393-9850
Hours Open	8 AM - 8 PM
Average Green Fees	$7/$12 wkdays, $8/$14 wkends
Special Rates?	Senior Citizens
Credit Cards	No
Season	May 1 - October 15
Amenities	Bar, course may be played as an 18, different tee markers for the same 9 greens-par 70
Dress Code	No
Tee Time Required?	No
Golf Packages Available?	No
10% discount available?	No

Validation_____Score_____Date_____

# of Holes	9	Par	35	Carts	YES	Clubs	YES

Potsdam Town & Country

Colton Rd. #56 • Zip 13676

Phone	(315) 265-8460
Hours Open	7 AM - dark
Average Green Fees	$16 wkdays, $18 wkends
Special Rates?	No
Credit Cards	MC/VISA
Season	April 15 - October 15
Amenities	Pro shop, lessons, bar, restaurant, driving range
Dress Code	Shirts & shoes must be worn at all times
Tee Time Required?	Reoommended
Golf Packages Available?	
10% discount available?	

Validation_____Score_____Date_____

# of Holes	9	Par	36	Carts	$18	Clubs	$3.50

Cedar View Golf Course

Route 370 • Zip 13683

Phone	(315) 764-9104
Hours Open	Daylight hours
Average Green Fees	$10 wkdays, $12 wkends
Special Rates?	No
Credit Cards	MC/VISA
Season	May - October
Amenities	Pro shop, lessons, bar, restaurant
Dress Code	Yes
Tee Time Required?	No
Golf Packages Available?	No
10% discount available?	Yes

Validation_____Score_____Date_____

# of Holes	18	Par	72	Carts	$18	Clubs	$3

Star Lake

Clifton Fine Golf Course

Main St. Route 3 • Zip 13690

Phone	(315) 848-3570
Hours Open	Daylight hours
Average Green Fees	$9.50 - $10.50
Special Rates?	On memberships only
Credit Cards	No
Season	Last week of April - 1 st week of October
Amenities	Pro shop, snack bar, practice green
Dress Code	Proper golf attire
Tee Time Required?	No
Golf Packages Available?	No
10% discount available?	Inquire

Validation_____Score_____Date_____

# of Holes	9	Par	36	Carts	$9/$18	Clubs	$5

Waddington

Twin Brooks 18 Hole

Franklin Rd. • Zip 13694

Phone	(315) 384-4126
Hours Open	Daylight hours
Average Green Fees	$12 wkdays, $15 wkends & holidays
Special Rates?	No
Credit Cards	No
Season	April - end of OCtober
Amenities	Pro shop, bar, restaurant, custom made clubs
Dress Code	Shirts required
Tee Time Required?	No
Golf Packages Available?	No
10% discount available?	Inquire

Validation_____Score_____Date_____

# of Holes	18	Par	71	Carts	$16	Clubs	$5

Winthrop

Meadowbrook Golf

Route 1 • Zip 13697

Phone	(315) 389-4562
Hours Open	Daylight hours
Average Green Fees	$10 and under
Special Rates?	Senior Citizens
Credit Cards	No
Season	April - October
Amenities	Pro shop, lessons, bar, restaurant, driving range
Dress Code	Shirts must be worn at all times
Tee Time Required?	Sundays, recommended
Golf Packages Available?	No
10% discount available?	Inquire

Validation_____Score_____Date_____

# of Holes	9	Par	36	Carts	$15	Clubs	$4

Addison

Pinnacle Golf Course

RD #1 Box 189 Ackerson Rd. • Zip 14801

Phone	(607) 359-2767
Hours Open	7 AM -dusk
Average Green Fees	$8/$12 wkdays, $9/$14 wkends
Special Rates?	NYS senior & junior residents M-F 1/2 price
Credit Cards	No
Season	April 10 - November
Amenities	Bar & restaurant, picnic area, hiking trails, cross-country skking in winter, driving range, magnificent view from clubhouse
Dress Code	Shirts must be worn at all times
Tee Time Required?	Yes-wkends, holidays, tournaments
Golf Packages Available?	Yes-green fees/golf cart
10% discount available?	Inquire

Validation_____Score_____Date_____

# of Holes	9	Par	36	Carts	YES	Clubs	YES

Hornell

Hornell Country Club

Seneca Rd. • Zip 14843

Phone	(607) 324-1735
Hours Open	7:30 AM - dusk
Average Green Fees	$12/18 wkdays, $14/18 wkends
Special Rates?	Call for details
Credit Cards	MC/VISA/DISC
Season	May 1 - October 15
Amenities	Pro shop, lessons, bar & restaurant
Dress Code	Shorts permitted, no tank tops
Tee Time Required?	Holidays only
Golf Packages Available?	Yes-wkends
10% discount available?	No

Validation_____Score_____Date_____

# of Holes	9	Par	71	Carts	$8/$15	Clubs	$1

Hornell

Twin Hickory Golf Club
1799 Turnpike Rd. • Zip 14843

Phone	(607) 324-1441
Hours Open	Daylight hours
Average Green Fees	$8/$11 wkdays, $9/$12 wkends
Special Rates?	Wkends after 3 PM
Credit Cards	No
Season	Mid April - November
Amenities	Pro shop, bar & restaurant
Dress Code	Shirts must be worn at all times
Tee Time Required?	No
Golf Packages Available?	No
10% discount available?	Inquire

Validation_____Score_____Date_____

# of Holes	18	Par	72	Carts	$16	Clubs	YES

Lindley

Indian Hills Golf Club
150 Indian Hills Rd. • Zip 14858

Phone	(607) 523-7315
Hours Open	Daylight hours
Average Green Fees	$18
Special Rates?	
Credit Cards	Yes
Season	Year round
Amenities	Bar & restaurant
Dress Code	No tank tops, proper golf attire
Tee Time Required?	Wkends only - call for course availability
Golf Packages Available?	No
10% discount available?	No

Validation_____Score_____Date_____

# of Holes	18	Par	72	Carts		Clubs	$7

Babylon

Robert Moses St. Pk. G.C.
Robert Moses State Park • Zip 11702

Phone	(516) 669-0449
Hours Open	7 AM - 6 PM
Average Green Fees	$10 and under
Special Rates?	Senior Citizens
Credit Cards	No
Season	April - September
Amenities	
Dress Code	No
Tee Time Required?	No
Golf Packages Available?	
10% discount available?	Inquire

Validation_____Score_____Date_____

# of Holes	18	Par	55	Carts	NO	Clubs	YES

Brentwood

Brentwood Country Club
Pennsylvania Ave. • Zip 11717

Phone	(516) 436-6060
Hours Open	7 AM - 6 PM
Average Green Fees	$10/$20
Special Rates?	Inquire
Credit Cards	
Season	April - November
Amenities	Pro shop, bar, restaurant, chipping area, putting green, showers
Dress Code	Collared shirts, no short shorts
Tee Time Required?	Wkends
Golf Packages Available?	
10% discount available?	Inquire

Validation_____Score_____Date_____

# of Holes	18	Par	72	Carts	YES	Clubs	YES

Bridgehampton

Poxabogue Golf Course
Montauk Hwy. • Zip 11932

Phone	(516) 537-0025
Hours Open	7 AM -dusk
Average Green Fees	$7.50 (Mon-Thurs) $9.50 (Fri-Sun & holidays)
Special Rates?	No
Credit Cards	No
Season	April 1 - November 30
Amenities	Pro shop, lessons, restaurant, driving range, children's clinics
Dress Code	Shirts must be worn at all times
Tee Time Required?	No
Golf Packages Available?	No
10% discount available?	Yes

Validation_____Score_____Date_____

# of Holes	9	Par	30	Carts	PULL	Clubs	YES

Centereach

Heatherwood Golf Club
Port Jeff Nesconset Hwy. • Zip 11720

Phone	(516) 473-9000
Hours Open	Daylight hours
Average Green Fees	$16
Special Rates?	No
Credit Cards	No
Season	All year, weather permitting
Amenities	Pro shop, restaurant, bar, PGA slope 105 rating 62.1
Dress Code	Yes
Tee Time Required?	Yes
Golf Packages Available?	No
10% discount available?	No

Validation_____Score_____Date_____

# of Holes	18	Par	60	Carts	YES	Clubs	YES

Central Islip

Gullhaven Golf Club
Carleton Ave. on Gullhaven • Zip 11722

Phone	(516) 436-6059
Hours Open	Daylight hours
Average Green Fees	$12/$14 NYS Res. $15/$18 Non. Res.
Special Rates?	Senior Citizens $8 /$10 wkdays, after 3 PM
Credit Cards	No
Season	All year round
Amenities	Pro shop, snack bar
Dress Code	No
Tee Time Required?	No
Golf Packages Available?	No
10% discount available?	No

Validation_____Score_____Date_____

# of Holes	9	Par	71	Carts	$8/$16	Clubs	$10

Cutchogue

Cedars Golf Club
Case's Lane • Zip 11935

Phone	(516) 734-6363
Hours Open	Daylight hours
Average Green Fees	$5 and under
Special Rates?	Senior Citizens
Credit Cards	No
Season	April 1 - October 31
Amenities	Pro shop, lessons, chipping area, putting green, no alcoholic beverages allowed, no person under 7 yrs. old
Dress Code	No bathing suits, swim trunks, bare feet
Tee Time Required?	First come, first served
Golf Packages Available?	10 ticket book - $40
10% discount available?	No

Validation_____Score_____Date_____

# of Holes	9	Par	27	Carts	PULL	Clubs	YES

Dix Hills Country Club
527 Half Hollow Rd. • Zip 11746

Phone	(516) 271-4788
Hours Open	Daylight hours
Average Green Fees	$11 wkdays, $12 wkends
Special Rates?	Senior Citizens
Credit Cards	No
Season	Year round
Amenities	Pro shop, lessons, beer & soda bar, snack bar, putting green
Dress Code	Shirts w/collars, no cutoffs, no tank tops
Tee Time Required?	Appreciated - $2 per person to reserve
Golf Packages Available?	No
10% discount available?	Inquire

Validation_____Score_____Date_____

# of Holes	9	Par	35	Carts	PULL	Clubs	$5

Hollow Hills Country Club
49 Ryder Ave. • Zip 11746

Phone	(516) 242-0010
Hours Open	7 AM - 6 PM wkdays, 6 AM - 6 PM wkends
Average Green Fees	$10 and under
Special Rates?	Senior Citizens
Credit Cards	No
Season	Year round weather permitting
Amenities	Clubs, gas/hand carts, restaurant, catering, pro shop, putting green
Dress Code	No tank tops, no cut offs
Tee Time Required?	
Golf Packages Available?	No
10% discount available?	No

Validation_____Score_____Date_____

# of Holes	9	Par	35	Carts	YES	Clubs	YES

Greenport

Island's End Golf & C. C.

Route 5 • Zip 11944

Phone	(516) 477-9457
Hours Open	6 AM - dusk
Average Green Fees	$24/$30
Special Rates?	No
Credit Cards	No
Season	March - December
Amenities	Lessons, pro shop, restaurant, bar, driving range, putting green, chipping area
Dress Code	5" inseam shorts, either sleeves or collar shirts
Tee Time Required?	No, available at $5 a person
Golf Packages Available?	No
10% discount available?	No

Validation_____Score_____Date_____

# of Holes	18	Par	72	Carts	$12/seat	Clubs	YES

Kings Park

Sunken Meadow St. Pk. G.C.

PO Box 716 • Zip 11754

Phone	(516) 269-4333
Hours Open	Daylight hours
Average Green Fees	$10 and under
Special Rates?	Senior Citizens
Credit Cards	No
Season	March - November (closed Mondays)
Amenities	Pro shop, club rentals, pull carts, putting green, driving range, restaurant
Dress Code	
Tee Time Required?	Not taken
Golf Packages Available?	
10% discount available?	No

Validation_____Score_____Date_____

# of Holes	9/9/9	Par	36/36/35	Carts	PULL	Clubs	YES

Manorville

Pine Hills Country Club

162 Wading River Rd. • Zip 11949

Phone	(516) 234-1600
Hours Open	Daylight hours-Open to public M-F, Sat. after 2PM
Average Green Fees	$18 - $20
Special Rates?	AFter 1 PM $12 - $14
Credit Cards	For equipment only
Season	April 1 - October 31
Amenities	Driving range, bunkers, putting green, chipping green, lessons w/pro. Restaurant next door.
Dress Code	Collared shirts, no cutoffs
Tee Time Required?	No, but recommended
Golf Packages Available?	No
10% discount available?	No

Validation_____Score_____Date_____

# of Holes	18	Par	73	Carts	$14/$25	Clubs	NO

Manorville

Swan Lake Golf Club
388 River Rd. • Zip 11949

Phone	(516) 369-1818
Hours Open	6 AM - dusk
Average Green Fees	$20 - $30
Special Rates?	No
Credit Cards	No
Season	April - October
Amenities	Pro shop, restaurant, putting green
Dress Code	No
Tee Time Required?	No
Golf Packages Available?	
10% discount available?	Inquire

Validation_____Score_____Date_____

# of Holes	18	Par	72	Carts	YES	Clubs	YES

Middle Island

Middle Island Country Club
Yaphank Rd. • Zip 11953

Phone	(516) 924-5100
Hours Open	7 AM - dusk
Average Green Fees	$10 - $20
Special Rates?	No
Credit Cards	No
Season	Year round
Amenities	Pro shop, lessons, bar, restaurant
Dress Code	Collared shirt, no cutoffs
Tee Time Required?	No
Golf Packages Available?	No
10% discount available?	Inquire

Validation_____Score_____Date_____

# of Holes	9/9/9	Par	36/36/36	Carts	YES	Clubs	YES

Middle Island

Spring Lake Golf Club

Rt. 25 & Bartlett Rd. • Zip 11953

Phone	(516) 924-5115
Hours Open	Daylight hours
Average Green Fees	$22
Special Rates?	
Credit Cards	No
Season	All year round
Amenities	
Dress Code	Collared shirts must be worn at all times
Tee Time Required?	No
Golf Packages Available?	No
10% discount available?	No

Validation_____Score_____Date_____

# of Holes	9/18	Par	36/72	Carts	$12.50/$25	Clubs	$15

Montauk

Montauk Downs

S. Fairview Ave. • Zip 11954

Phone	(516) 668-5000
Hours Open	Daylight hours
Average Green Fees	$10 - $20
Special Rates?	After 4 PM
Credit Cards	Yes (pro shop only)
Season	March - December
Amenities	Pro shop, lessons, bar, restaurant, driving range, putting green
Dress Code	No
Tee Time Required?	No
Golf Packages Available?	Yes-thru pro shop & food concession
10% discount available?	No

Validation_____Score_____Date_____

# of Holes	18	Par	72	Carts	YES	Clubs	YES

Northport

Crab Meadow Golf Course
220 Waterside Ave. • Zip 11768

Phone	(516) 757-8831
Hours Open	6 AM - 6 PM
Average Green Fees	$10 - $20
Special Rates?	Inquire
Credit Cards	No
Season	March 19 - December 22
Amenities	Pro shop, lessons, bar, restaurant, chipping/putting area
Dress Code	No tank tops
Tee Time Required?	No
Golf Packages Available?	No
10% discount available?	Inquire

Validation_____Score_____Date_____

# of Holes	18	Par	72	Carts	$25	Clubs	$20-$30

Riverhead

Sandy Pond Golf Course
Roanoke Ave. • Zip 11901

Phone	(516) 727-0909
Hours Open	Daylight hours
Average Green Fees	$4/$5
Special Rates?	Senior Citizens $1 off
Credit Cards	No
Season	Year round (weather permitting)
Amenities	Snack & soda machines, lessons
Dress Code	No
Tee Time Required?	No
Golf Packages Available?	No
10% discount available?	No

Validation_____Score_____Date_____

# of Holes	9	Par	27	Carts	PULL	Clubs	YES

Rocky Point

Tall Tree Golf Course

Rt. 25A • Zip 11778

Phone	(516) 744-3200
Hours Open	6 AM - dusk
Average Green Fees	$10 - $20
Special Rates?	No
Credit Cards	No
Season	Year round
Amenities	Pro shop, lessons, restaurant, chipping/putting area
Dress Code	Proper attire
Tee Time Required?	Wkends only
Golf Packages Available?	No
10% discount available?	Inquire

Validation_____Score_____Date_____

# of Holes	18	Par	65	Carts	YES	Clubs	YES

Shelter Island Hts.

Shelter Island Country Club

26 Sunnyside Ave. • Zip 11964

Phone	(516) 749-0416
Hours Open	Daylight hours
Average Green Fees	$10 - $16
Special Rates?	No
Credit Cards	No
Season	May 1 - November 1
Amenities	Pro shop, snack bar, dining room, lessons available
Dress Code	Proper golf attire
Tee Time Required?	No
Golf Packages Available?	W/Shelter Island Resorts
10% discount available?	No

Validation_____Score_____Date_____

# of Holes	9	Par	32	Carts	$10/$16	Clubs	YES

Smithtown

Smithtown Landing C. C.
495 Landing Ave. • Zip 11787

Phone	(516) 360-7618
Hours Open	Daylight hours - Non-members Tu. - Fri. only
Average Green Fees	$10 - $20
Special Rates?	Wkend & wkdays - 9 hole rate
Credit Cards	No
Season	April 1 - November 1
Amenities	Pro shop, lessons, bar, restaurant
Dress Code	No cutoffs
Tee Time Required?	No
Golf Packages Available?	
10% discount available?	Inquire

Validation_____Score_____Date_____

# of Holes	9/18	Par	36/72	Carts	YES	Clubs	

West Babylon

Bergen Point
Bergen Ave. • Zip 11704

Phone	(516) 661-8282
Hours Open	Daylight hours
Average Green Fees	Res. $17, Non. Res. $20 - $22
Special Rates?	After 4 PM & Senior Citizens
Credit Cards	No
Season	March 15 - December 15
Amenities	Pro shop, lessons, driving range, snack bar, restaurant & bar
Dress Code	Collared shirts, no cutoffs
Tee Time Required?	No
Golf Packages Available?	No
10% discount available?	No

Validation_____Score_____Date_____

# of Holes	18	Par	71	Carts	$22	Clubs	YES

Callicoon

Villa Roma Country Club
Rt. 1 Villa Roma Rd. • Zip 12723

Phone	(914) 887-5097
Hours Open	7:30 AM - 6 PM
Average Green Fees	$20 - $30 wkdays
Special Rates?	Group rates available
Credit Cards	MC/VISA/AMEX
Season	April - November
Amenities	Pro shop, lessons, bar & restaurant
Dress Code	No tee shirts, no cut offs
Tee Time Required?	Yes
Golf Packages Available?	Yes
10% discount available?	Yes ($5 on green fees & cart)

Validation_____ Score_____ Date_____

# of Holes	18	Par	71	Carts	$25	Clubs	$10-$20

Ferndale

Grossinger Resort Corp.
St. Hwy. 52 • Zip 12734

Phone	(914) 292-9000
Hours Open	7 AM - 5 PM
Average Green Fees	Undetermined
Special Rates?	
Credit Cards	Undetermined
Season	April - October 31
Amenities	Lessons, pro shop, driving range, tennis, pool
Dress Code	Proper golf attire
Tee Time Required?	Yes
Golf Packages Available?	Rooms on premises
10% discount available?	No

Validation_____ Score_____ Date_____

# of Holes	27	Par	36/71	Carts	YES	Clubs	YES

Kiamesha Lake

The Concord - 3 Courses
Kiamesha Lake Rd. • Zip 12751

Phone	(914) 794-4000 ext. 3325
Hours Open	Daylight hours-7 AM - 6 PM
Average Green Fees	$20 - $90
Special Rates?	After 3:30 PM
Credit Cards	All major
Season	April - November
Amenities	Pro shop, lessons, bar & restaurant. The Challenger-9 hole par 31, The Monster-18 holes par 72, The International-18 holes par 71.
Dress Code	Proper golf attire
Tee Time Required?	Yes
Golf Packages Available?	Yes
10% discount available?	Inquire

Validation_____Score_____Date_____

# of Holes	9/18/18	Par	31/72/71	Carts	$15	Clubs	$10 - $25

Liberty

Bogey's
Rt. 52 • Zip 12754

Phone	(914) 292-3900
Hours Open	Daylight hours
Average Green Fees	$10 - $20
Special Rates?	After 5 PM wkdays, after 3 PM wkends & holidays
Credit Cards	No
Season	May 1 - October 31
Amenities	Restaurant, pro shop, alternate tees
Dress Code	Proper golf attire, shirts w/collars
Tee Time Required?	No
Golf Packages Available?	Yes-with certain hotels in area
10% discount available?	No

Validation_____Score_____Date_____

# of Holes	9	Par	72	Carts	$12-$20	Clubs	YES

Liberty

Sullivan County G.C.

Rt. 52 • Zip 12754

Phone	(914) 292-9584
Hours Open	Daylight hours
Average Green Fees	$10 and under
Special Rates?	Wkdays
Credit Cards	No
Season	
Amenities	Pro shop, lessons, bar & restaurant
Dress Code	Collared shirts
Tee Time Required?	No
Golf Packages Available?	
10% discount available?	Inquire

Validation_____Score_____Date_____

# of Holes	9	Par	72	Carts	$15	Clubs	NO

Loch Sheldrake

Lochmor Golf Club

Hurleyville-Loch Sheldrake • Zip 12759

Phone	(914) 434-9079
Hours Open	Daylight hours
Average Green Fees	$18
Special Rates?	Afer 1 PM
Credit Cards	No
Season	
Amenities	Pro shop, lessons, bar & restaurant
Dress Code	Proper attire
Tee Time Required?	Wkends
Golf Packages Available?	No
10% discount available?	Inquire

Validation_____Score_____Date_____

# of Holes	18	Par	72	Carts	$22	Clubs	$5 - $10

Monticello

Kutsher's Country Club

Kutsher Rd. • Zip 12701

Phone	(914) 794-6000
Hours Open	Daylight hours
Average Green Fees	$20 - $30
Special Rates?	
Credit Cards	Yes
Season	April - November
Amenities	Pro shop, lessons, bar, restaurant, driving range
Dress Code	Yes
Tee Time Required?	Yes
Golf Packages Available?	Yes
10% discount available?	Inquire

Validation_____Score_____Date_____

# of Holes	18	Par	71	Carts	YES	Clubs	YES

Roscoe

Tennanah Lake Golf Club

Hankins Rd. • Zip 12776

Phone	(607) 498-5502
Hours Open	Daylight hours
Average Green Fees	$10 and under
Special Rates?	Wkdays
Credit Cards	MC/VISA/AMEX
Season	
Amenities	Pro shop, food only
Dress Code	Collared shirts
Tee Time Required?	Yes
Golf Packages Available?	Yes
10% discount available?	Inquire

Validation_____Score_____Date_____

# of Holes	18	Par	72	Carts	$15	Clubs	$5

Roscoe

Twin Village Golf Club
Rockland Rd. • Zip 12776

Phone	(607) 498-9983
Hours Open	Daylight hours
Average Green Fees	$10 and under
Special Rates?	Wkdays
Credit Cards	
Season	
Amenities	Food only
Dress Code	
Tee Time Required?	
Golf Packages Available?	
10% discount available?	Inquire

Validation_____Score_____Date_____

# of Holes	9	Par	32	Carts	$15	Clubs	

S. Fallsburg

Tarry Brae Golf Course
Pleasant Valley Rd. • Zip 12779

Phone	(914) 434-2622
Hours Open	Daylight hours
Average Green Fees	$18
Special Rates?	Wkdays
Credit Cards	No
Season	
Amenities	Pro shop, lessons, bar, restaurant
Dress Code	Yes
Tee Time Required?	No
Golf Packages Available?	Yes
10% discount available?	Inquire

Validation_____Score_____Date_____

# of Holes	18	Par	72	Carts	$22	Clubs	$4 - $7

S. Fallsburg

The Pines

Laurel Rd.• Zip 12779

Phone	(914) 434-6000
Hours Open	Daylight hours
Average Green Fees	$10 and under
Special Rates?	After 3 PM
Credit Cards	MC/VISA
Season	
Amenities	Pro shop, lessons
Dress Code	Proper attire
Tee Time Required?	Yes
Golf Packages Available?	
10% discount available?	Inquire

Validation_____Score_____Date_____

# of Holes	9	Par	32	Carts	$15	Clubs	$6

Spring Glen

Homowack Lodge

Old Route 209 Box 369 • Zip 12483

Phone	(914) 647-6800
Hours Open	Daylight hours
Average Green Fees	$8 - $10
Special Rates?	No
Credit Cards	No
Season	April - November
Amenities	Pro shop, lessons
Dress Code	Casual
Tee Time Required?	Yes (w/starter)
Golf Packages Available?	No
10% discount available?	No

Validation_____Score_____Date_____

# of Holes	9	Par	36	Carts	YES	Clubs	YES

Swan Lake

Swan Lake Golf & C.C.

Stevensville Rd. • Zip 12783

Phone	(914) 292-0323
Hours Open	7 AM - 5:30 PM
Average Green Fees	$15/$25
Special Rates?	No
Credit Cards	MC/VISA/AMEX
Season	May - November (weather permitting)
Amenities	Pro shop, bar, snack bar, driving range, putting green
Dress Code	Proper golf attire
Tee Time Required?	Yes
Golf Packages Available?	No
10% discount available?	Yes

Validation_____Score_____Date_____

# of Holes	18	Par	72	Carts	$20/$30	Clubs	$8

Apalachin

Apalachin Golf Course
S. Apalachin Rd. • Zip 13732

Phone	(607) 625-2682
Hours Open	Daylight hours
Average Green Fees	$7 wkdays, $10 wkends & holidays
Special Rates?	Senior Citizens, juniors
Credit Cards	
Season	April - November (weather permitting)
Amenities	Pro shop, bar, restaurant
Dress Code	Shirts must be worn at all times
Tee Time Required?	No
Golf Packages Available?	No
10% discount available?	Inquire

Validation_____Score_____Date_____

# of Holes	9	Par	36	Carts	$14/$18	Clubs	YES

Berkshire

Grandview Farms G.C.
400 Hartwell Rd. • Zip 13736

Phone	(607) 657-2619
Hours Open	Daylight hours
Average Green Fees	$5 wkdays, $6 wkends & holidays
Special Rates?	Yes
Credit Cards	MC/VISA
Season	April 1 - November 15
Amenities	Bed & breakfast
Dress Code	No
Tee Time Required?	No
Golf Packages Available?	Yes
10% discount available?	Yes (on wkdays only)

Validation_____Score_____Date_____

# of Holes	9	Par	35	Carts	YES	Clubs	YES

Candor

Catatonk Golf Club
71 Golf Club Rd. • Zip 13743

Phone	(607) 659-4600
Hours Open	Daylight hours
Average Green Fees	$10 wkdays, $12 wkends
Special Rates?	4 golfers w/2 carts & breakfast for $60
Credit Cards	No
Season	May - October
Amenities	Pro shop, bar, restaurant
Dress Code	Shts must be worn at all times
Tee Time Required?	Yes
Golf Packages Available?	
10% discount available?	No

Validation_____Score_____Date_____

# of Holes	18	Par	72	Carts	YES	Clubs	NO

Newark Valley

Newark Valley Golf Course
RR 38N Box 223 • Zip 13811

Phone	(607) 642-3376
Hours Open	Daylight hours
Average Green Fees	$9 - $11
Special Rates?	Senior Citizens - wkdays
Credit Cards	No
Season	
Amenities	Pro shop, food only
Dress Code	Shirts
Tee Time Required?	Wkends
Golf Packages Available?	
10% discount available?	Inquire

Validation_____Score_____Date_____

# of Holes	18	Par	68	Carts	YES	Clubs	NO

Nichols

Tioga Country Club
Ro-Ki Blvd. • Zip 13812

Phone	(607) 699-3881
Hours Open	7 AM - 7 PM
Average Green Fees	$11 - $15
Special Rates?	Wkends before 1 PM - 2 green fees & cart $30
Credit Cards	No
Season	April 1 - October 31
Amenities	Pro shop, lessons, bar, restaurant
Dress Code	No tank tops
Tee Time Required?	Recommended
Golf Packages Available?	
10% discount available?	No

Validation_____Score_____Date_____

# of Holes	18	Par	71	Carts	$10/$18	Clubs	$5

Waverly

D J's Golf Center
5974 Old Rt. 17 • Zip 14892

Phone	(607) 565-2618
Hours Open	8 Am - 9 PM wkdays, 7:30 AM - 9PM wkends
Average Green Fees	$10 and under
Special Rates?	No
Credit Cards	Yes
Season	March - November
Amenities	Full top line pro shop, driving range, mini-golf, ice cream parlor, lessons (group, private, junior program)
Dress Code	Shirts & shoes at all times
Tee Time Required?	No
Golf Packages Available?	Yes
10% discount available?	No

Validation_____Score_____Date_____

# of Holes	9	Par	27	Carts	NO	Clubs	YES

Dryden

Dryden Lake Golf Course
430 Lake Rd. • Zip 13053

Phone	(607) 844-9173
Hours Open	Daylight hours
Average Green Fees	$10 wkdays, $12 wkends
Special Rates?	Senior Citizens $8 wkdays
Credit Cards	No
Season	April 1 - October 31
Amenities	Pro shop, lessons, bar, restaurant, driving range, putting green, pitching green
Dress Code	Shirts must be worn at all times
Tee Time Required?	Recommended
Golf Packages Available?	Wkday golf & lunch special
10% discount available?	Yes

Validation_____Score_____Date_____

# of Holes	9	Par	33	Carts	$9/$18	Clubs	$5

Groton

Stonehedges Golf Club
Lick St. • Zip 13073

Phone	(607) 898-3754
Hours Open	7 AM - dusk
Average Green Fees	$10 and under
Special Rates?	Wkdays
Credit Cards	No
Season	
Amenities	Pro shop, bar, restaurant
Dress Code	Shirts
Tee Time Required?	No
Golf Packages Available?	
10% discount available?	Inquire

Validation_____Score_____Date_____

# of Holes	18	Par	72	Carts	$15/$25	Clubs	$5

Ithaca

Hillendale Golf Course

218 Applegate Rd. N. • Zip 14850

Phone	(607) 273-2363
Hours Open	Daylight hours
Average Green Fees	$12
Special Rates?	Wkdays
Credit Cards	MC/VISA
Season	April - October
Amenities	Pro shop, lessons, bar, restaurant
Dress Code	Shirts must be worn at all times
Tee Time Required?	No
Golf Packages Available?	
10% discount available?	Yes

Validation_____Score_____Date_____

# of Holes	18	Par	71	Carts	$16	Clubs	$5

Ithaca

Newman Golf Course

10 Pier Rd. • Zip 14850

Phone	(607) 273-6262
Hours Open	7 AM - dusk
Average Green Fees	$10
Special Rates?	Senior Citizens
Credit Cards	Yes, pro shop only
Season	April - November
Amenities	Pro shop, lessons, bar only, showers, lockers
Dress Code	Sht and shoes required at all times
Tee Time Required?	Wkends only
Golf Packages Available?	No
10% discount available?	Inquire

Validation_____Score_____Date_____

# of Holes	9	Par	36	Carts	$8/$14	Clubs	$5

Trumansburg

Trumansburg Golf Club

Halsey St. • Zip 14886

Phone	(607) 387-8844
Hours Open	Daylight hours
Average Green Fees	$14
Special Rates?	Senior Citizens
Credit Cards	MC/VISA
Season	
Amenities	Pro shop, lessons, bar, restaurant
Dress Code	No
Tee Time Required?	Wkends only
Golf Packages Available?	
10% discount available?	Inquire

Validation_____Score_____Date_____

# of Holes	9	Par	36	Carts	YES	Clubs	$5

Accord

Rondout Country Club	Whitfield Rd. • Zip12404

Phone	(914) 626-2513
Hours Open	7 AM - dusk
Average Green Fees	$20 - $30
Special Rates?	No
Credit Cards	MC/VISA/AMEX
Season	April - September
Amenities	Restaurant, bar, pro shop, tennis courts, swimming pool, driving range
Dress Code	No tank tops
Tee Time Required?	No
Golf Packages Available?	No
10% discount available?	No

Validation_____Score_____Date_____

# of Holes	18	Par	72	Carts	INCL	Clubs	YES

Ellenville

Fallsview	Nevele Rd. off Rt. 209 • Zip 12428

Phone	(914) 647-5100
Hours Open	Daylight hours
Average Green Fees	$10 - $20
Special Rates?	After 3 PM
Credit Cards	MC/VISA/AMEX
Season	April - November
Amenities	Pro shop, lessons, bar, restaurant, hotel
Dress Code	Shirts must be worn , no tank tops or short shorts
Tee Time Required?	Yes
Golf Packages Available?	
10% discount available?	Inquire

Validation_____Score_____Date_____

# of Holes	9	Par	35	Carts	YES	Clubs	YES

Ellenville

Nevele Country Club
Nevele Rd. • Zip 12428

Phone	(914) 647-7315
Hours Open	Daylight hours
Average Green Fees	$10 and under
Special Rates?	Wkdays
Credit Cards	MC/VISA
Season	
Amenities	Pro shop, lessons, bar, restaurant
Dress Code	Collared shirts, no jeans
Tee Time Required?	Yes
Golf Packages Available?	Yes
10% discount available?	Inquire

Validation_____Score_____Date_____

# of Holes	18	Par	70	Carts	$15	Clubs	$12

Ellenville

Shawangunk Country Club
Nevele Rd. • Zip 12428

Phone	(914) 647-6090
Hours Open	7 AM - dusk
Average Green Fees	$8/$12 wkdays, $10/$15 wkends
Special Rates?	Groups
Credit Cards	No
Season	April 1 - Ocober 31
Amenities	Golf shop, dining room, putting green
Dress Code	Yes
Tee Time Required?	Recommended wkdays,, required wkends
Golf Packages Available?	No, honor Golf Card International & Hale Irwin
10% discount available?	No

Validation_____Score_____Date_____

# of Holes	9	Par	34	Carts	YES	Clubs	YES

High Falls

Stone Dock Golf Course

Berme Rd. • Zip 12440

Phone	(914) 687-9944
Hours Open	Daylight hours
Average Green Fees	Call for details
Special Rates?	No
Credit Cards	MC/VISA
Season	March - November
Amenities	Restaurant, bar, pro shop
Dress Code	No
Tee Time Required?	No
Golf Packages Available?	No
10% discount available?	No

Validation_____Score_____Date_____

# of Holes	9	Par	36	Carts	YES	Clubs	YES

Kerhonkson

Granit

Granit Road • Zip 12446

Phone	(914) 626-3141
Hours Open	Daylight hours
Average Green Fees	$10 and under
Special Rates?	Wkdays
Credit Cards	Yes
Season	April - November
Amenities	Pro shop, lessons, bar & restaurant, hotel
Dress Code	Shirts must be worn at all times
Tee Time Required?	No
Golf Packages Available?	Yes
10% discount available?	Inquire

Validation_____Score_____Date_____

# of Holes	18	Par	70	Carts	$15	Clubs	YES

Green Acres Golf Club   Harwich St. • Zip 12401

Phone	(914) 331-2283
Hours Open	7 AM - 7 PM
Average Green Fees	$5 - $10
Special Rates?	No
Credit Cards	No
Season	April - November
Amenities	
Dress Code	Shirts must be worn at all times
Tee Time Required?	No
Golf Packages Available?	No
10% discount available?	Yes

Validation_____Score_____Date_____

# of Holes	9	Par	36	Carts	YES	Clubs	YES

New Paltz

Mohonk Golf Course
Lake Mohonk • Zip 12561

Phone	(914) 255-1000
Hours Open	7:30 AM - dusk
Average Green Fees	$10
Special Rates?	Senior Citizens, M-F morning special
Credit Cards	MC/VISA/AMEX
Season	Early April - mid November
Amenities	Restaurant, resort, tennis, beach, affiliated w/Mohonk Mountain House Resort
Dress Code	No tank tops or short shorts
Tee Time Required?	Wkends & holidays
Golf Packages Available?	Corporate groups & large groups
10% discount available?	Yes

Validation_____Score_____Date_____

# of Holes	9	Par	35	Carts	YES	Clubs	YES

Saugerties

Katsbaan Golf Club
1754 Kings Hwy. • Zip 12477

Phone	(914) 246-8182
Hours Open	7:30 AM - dusk
Average Green Fees	$7.50/$10
Special Rates?	Season membership
Credit Cards	No
Season	April - October
Amenities	Snack bar, pro shop, bar, lessons, cheerful service
Dress Code	Proper golf attire
Tee Time Required?	Recommended
Golf Packages Available?	No
10% discount available?	Yes

Validation_____Score_____Date_____

# of Holes	9/9	Par	70	Carts	YES	Clubs	YES

Walker Valley

Walker Valley Golf Club

Rt. 52 • Zip 12588

Phone	(914) 744-5211
Hours Open	Daylight hours
Average Green Fees	$6 wkdays, $8 wkends & holidays
Special Rates?	Senior Citizens
Credit Cards	
Season	April 1 - November 1
Amenities	Pro shop, restaurant
Dress Code	Proper golf attire
Tee Time Required?	Wkends
Golf Packages Available?	No
10% discount available?	Inquire

Validation_____Score_____Date_____

# of Holes	EXEC 9	Par		Carts	PULL	Clubs	$4

Bolton Landing

Sagamore Golf Club
Federal Hill Rd. • Zip 12814

Phone	(518) 644-9400
Hours Open	Daylight hours
Average Green Fees	$65
Special Rates?	No
Credit Cards	MC/VISA
Season	April - November
Amenities	Pro shop, restaurant, 3 day unlimited golf $150 May-June 15 only thru Sagamore Hotel
Dress Code	Yes
Tee Time Required?	Recommended
Golf Packages Available?	Call for details
10% discount available?	Inquire

Validation_____Score_____Date_____

# of Holes	18	Par	70	Carts	$17	Clubs	YES

Chestertown

Green Mansions
Darrowsville Rd. • Zip 12817

Phone	(518) 494-7222
Hours Open	8 AM - dark
Average Green Fees	$10/$20
Special Rates?	Wkdays after 5 PM
Credit Cards	No
Season	May 1 - October 30
Amenities	Driving range, practice green, lessons, pro shop, restaurant
Dress Code	No
Tee Time Required?	No
Golf Packages Available?	No
10% discount available?	Inquire

Validation_____Score_____Date_____

# of Holes	9	Par	36	Carts	$15/$25	Clubs	YES

Glens Falls

Bay Meadows Golf Club
Cronin Rd. • Zip 12801

Phone	(518) 792-1650
Hours Open	Daylight hours
Average Green Fees	$8 - $12
Special Rates?	No
Credit Cards	No
Season	May - November
Amenities	Driving range, practice green, lessons, pro shop, restaurant
Dress Code	Shirts required
Tee Time Required?	No
Golf Packages Available?	No
10% discount available?	Inquire

Validation_____Score_____Date_____

# of Holes	9	Par	35	Carts	$10 - $15	Clubs	YES

Lake George

Queensbury County Club
Route 149 • Zip 12845

Phone	(518) 793-3711
Hours Open	6 AM - dusk
Average Green Fees	$10/$20
Special Rates?	No
Credit Cards	MC/VISA
Season	April - November
Amenities	Driving range, practice green, lessons, pro shop, restaurant
Dress Code	Shirts required
Tee Time Required?	Usually
Golf Packages Available?	No
10% discount available?	Inquire

Validation_____Score_____Date_____

# of Holes	18	Par	70	Carts	$10 - $20	Clubs	YES

Lake George

Top of the World
Lockhart Mt. Rd. E. Side • Zip 12845

Phone	(518) 668-2062
Hours Open	7 AM - dusk
Average Green Fees	$12 - $17
Special Rates?	After 4 PM
Credit Cards	No
Season	May 1 - November 1
Amenities	Lessons, pro shop, bar, snack bar, club house
Dress Code	Shirts required
Tee Time Required?	No
Golf Packages Available?	Yes - Overlook Tours pkg.
10% discount available?	Inquire

Validation_____Score_____Date_____

# of Holes	9	Par	36	Carts	$10/$19	Clubs	YES

Queensbury

Hiland Park Golf Club
67 Haviland Rd. • Zip 12804

Phone	(518)761-GOLF
Hours Open	6 AM - dark
Average Green Fees	$25 - $35
Special Rates?	After 3 PM
Credit Cards	MC/VISA/AMEX
Season	April 1 - 1st snowfall
Amenities	Snack bar, restaurant, practice green, driving range
Dress Code	Shirts with collars
Tee Time Required?	At all times
Golf Packages Available?	For Golf & Dine
10% discount available?	No

Validation_____Score_____Date_____

# of Holes	18	Par	72	Carts	$15	Clubs	YES

Queensbury

Sunnyside
Sunnyside Rd. • Zip 12801

Phone	(518) 792-0148
Hours Open	7:30 AM - dusk
Average Green Fees	$7 - $8
Special Rates?	Senior Citizens
Credit Cards	No
Season	April 15 - November
Amenities	Restaurant
Dress Code	No
Tee Time Required?	No
Golf Packages Available?	No
10% discount available?	Inquire

Validation_____Score_____Date_____

# of Holes	9	Par	3	Carts	NO	Clubs	YES

Stony Creek

1000 Acres Golf Club
Rt. 418 • Zip 12878

Phone	(518) 696-5246
Hours Open	7 AM - dusk
Average Green Fees	$14 and under
Special Rates?	Senior Citizens
Credit Cards	MC/VISA
Season	May - November 1
Amenities	Driving range, practice green, lessons, pro shop, restaurant
Dress Code	Proper golf attire
Tee Time Required?	Wkends
Golf Packages Available?	Yes, groups
10% discount available?	Inquire

Validation_____Score_____Date_____

# of Holes	9	Par		Carts	$18	Clubs	YES

Warrensburg

Cronin's Golf Resort

Golf Course Rd. • Zip 12885

Phone	(518) 623-9336
Hours Open	6:30 AM - dusk
Average Green Fees	$12 - $20
Special Rates?	Wed. morning
Credit Cards	No
Season	April - November
Amenities	Practice green, lessons, pro shop, restaurant, pool, motel
Dress Code	No
Tee Time Required?	Wkends
Golf Packages Available?	
10% discount available?	Inquire

Validation_____Score_____Date_____

# of Holes	18	Par	70	Carts	$18	Clubs	YES

Fort Edward

Wedgewood Par 3 G.C.

East Rd. • Zip 12828

Phone	(518) 747-0003
Hours Open	9 AM - 9 PM
Average Green Fees	$5
Special Rates?	Senior Citizens
Credit Cards	No
Season	April - October
Amenities	Cocktail bar
Dress Code	Casual
Tee Time Required?	No
Golf Packages Available?	Yes
10% discount available?	Inquire

Validation_____Score_____Date_____

# of Holes	9	Par	27	Carts	NO	Clubs	YES

Hudson Falls

Kingswood Golf Club

Notre Dame Ext. • Zip 12839

Phone	(518) 747-888
Hours Open	7 AM - dusk
Average Green Fees	$20 - $26
Special Rates?	Senior Citizens
Credit Cards	MC/VISA
Season	May 1 - November
Amenities	Lessons, grill room, pro shop, driving range, PGA Golf instruction
Dress Code	Proper golf attire
Tee Time Required?	Yes
Golf Packages Available?	With Overlook Tours
10% discount available?	$1 off green fees

Validation_____Score_____Date_____

# of Holes	18	Par	71	Carts	$11	Clubs	YES

Hulett's Landing

Hulett's Golf Course

Off Rt. 6 • Zip 12841

Phone	(518) 499-1234
Hours Open	Daylight hours
Average Green Fees	$6 Monday - Saturday, $7 Sundays
Special Rates?	No
Credit Cards	No
Season	May 30 - Labor Day
Amenities	
Dress Code	No
Tee Time Required?	No
Golf Packages Available?	No
10% discount available?	Yes

Validation_____Score_____Date_____

# of Holes	9	Par	33	Carts	NO	Clubs	NO

Whitehall

Skene Valley C. C.

RD #2 Box 2975 • Zip 12887

Phone	(518) 499-1685
Hours Open	Daylight hours
Average Green Fees	$15
Special Rates?	
Credit Cards	No
Season	April - November (weather permitting)
Amenities	Pro shop, lessons, bar & restaurant
Dress Code	No muscle shirts, cutoffs, half shirts
Tee Time Required?	No
Golf Packages Available?	No
10% discount available?	No

Validation_____Score_____Date_____

# of Holes	18	Par	72	Carts	YES	Clubs	YES

Lyons

Wayne Hills Golf Course
2250 Gannett Rd. • Zip 14489

Phone	(315) 946-6944
Hours Open	Daylight hours
Average Green Fees	$30
Special Rates?	No
Credit Cards	No
Season	April 1 - November 1
Amenities	Pro shop, lessons, bar, restaurant, putting green, driving range
Dress Code	No cutoffs or tank tops
Tee Time Required?	Yes
Golf Packages Available?	No
10% discount available?	No

Validation_____Score_____Date_____

# of Holes	18	Par	72	Carts	$10	Clubs	NO

Macedon

Marvin's Restrnt & Party
1148 Wayneport Rd. • Zip 14502

Phone	(315) 986-4455
Hours Open	7 AM - 9 PM wkdays, 6 AM - 9 PM wkends
Average Green Fees	$10/$16 wkdays, $11/$18 wkends
Special Rates?	
Credit Cards	No
Season	March 15 - October 31
Amenities	
Dress Code	Yes
Tee Time Required?	Wkends & holidays
Golf Packages Available?	Memberships
10% discount available?	Yes

Validation_____Score_____Date_____

# of Holes	18	Par	70	Carts	$8/$16	Clubs	$5

Newark

Taranwould Public Golf

2084 Hydesville Rd. • Zip 14513

Phone	(315) 331-9128
Hours Open	8 AM - dusk, 6 AM - dusk in July & August, per tee time on wkends
Average Green Fees	$8.50/$13.50
Special Rates?	Large groups
Credit Cards	MC/VISA
Season	April - December 24th
Amenities	Meals on wkends
Dress Code	Yes
Tee Time Required?	Wkends
Golf Packages Available?	Yes
10% discount available?	Yes

Validation_____Score_____Date_____

# of Holes	18	Par	61	Carts	YES	Clubs	YES

Sodus Point

Sodus Bay Heights Golf Club

Bayview Dr. • Zip 14555

Phone	(315) 483-6777
Hours Open	Daylight hours
Average Green Fees	$25
Special Rates?	No
Credit Cards	No
Season	
Amenities	Pro shop, lessons, bar, restaurant
Dress Code	Casual
Tee Time Required?	Yes
Golf Packages Available?	No
10% discount available?	No

Validation_____Score_____Date_____

# of Holes	18	Par	72	Carts	YES	Clubs	NO

Walworth

Blue Heron Hills C.C.

1 Country Club Dr. • Zip 14568

Phone	(315) 986-2007
Hours Open	Daylight hours
Average Green Fees	$20 - $30 wjdays
Special Rates?	Wkends
Credit Cards	MC/VISA
Season	April 1 - December 1 (weather permitting)
Amenities	Pro shop, lessons, bar, restaurant
Dress Code	No jeans, golf shirts w/collars, no short shorts
Tee Time Required?	No
Golf Packages Available?	No
10% discount available?	No

Validation_____Score_____Date_____

# of Holes	18	Par	71	Carts	$10	Clubs	$10-$20

Wolcott

Port Bay Golf Club

7430 E. Part Bay Rd. • Zip 14590

Phone	(315) 594-8295
Hours Open	7 AM - dusk
Average Green Fees	$8/$10 wkdays, $10/$12 wkends
Special Rates?	$6 after 6 PM, with cart $13
Credit Cards	No
Season	April - October (weather permitting)
Amenities	Pro shop
Dress Code	Shirts must be worn at all times
Tee Time Required?	No
Golf Packages Available?	
10% discount available?	Yes

Validation_____Score_____Date_____

# of Holes	9	Par	35	Carts	$8/$16	Clubs	YES

Scarsdale

Saxon Woods Golf Course
Mamaroneck Rd. • Zip 10583

Phone	(914) 723-0949
Hours Open	6:30 AM - 7 PM wkdays, 5:30 AM - 7 PM wkends
Average Green Fees	Res. $12/$15, Non. Res. $35/$40
Special Rates?	Senior Citizens
Credit Cards	Yes, thru 285-GOLF
Season	April - December 15
Amenities	Restaurant, pro shop, halfway house, lockers, showers
Dress Code	No tank tops
Tee Time Required?	Recommended
Golf Packages Available?	No
10% discount available?	No

Validation_____Score_____Date_____

# of Holes	18	Par	71	Carts	$20	Clubs	YES

Shrub Oak

Indian Valley
Zip 10588

Phone	(914) 245-9816
Hours Open	Daylight hours
Average Green Fees	
Special Rates?	
Credit Cards	
Season	
Amenities	Bar, restaurant
Dress Code	
Tee Time Required?	
Golf Packages Available?	
10% discount available?	Inquire

Validation_____Score_____Date_____

# of Holes	9	Par	27	Carts		Clubs	

White Plains

Maple Moor Golf Course
North Street • Zip 10601

Phone	(914) 949-6752
Hours Open	6:30 AM - 7 PM wkdays, 5:30 AM - 7 PM wkends
Average Green Fees	Res. $12/$15, Non. Res. $35/$40
Special Rates?	Senior Citizens
Credit Cards	Yes, thru 285-GOLF
Season	April - December 15
Amenities	Restaurant, pro shop, lessons, showers, lockers
Dress Code	No tank tops
Tee Time Required?	Recommended
Golf Packages Available?	No
10% discount available?	No

Validation_____Score_____Date_____

# of Holes	18	Par		Carts	YES	Clubs	YES

Yonkers

Dunwoodie Golf Course
Wasylenko Lane • Zip 10701

Phone	(914) 476-5151
Hours Open	Daylight hours
Average Green Fees	Res. $12/$15, Non. Res. $35/$40
Special Rates?	Senior Citizens
Credit Cards	Yes, thru 285-GOLF
Season	April - December 15
Amenities	Restaurant, lounge, pro shop, showers, lockers, driving range
Dress Code	Shirts required at all times
Tee Time Required?	Recommended
Golf Packages Available?	No
10% discount available?	No

Validation_____Score_____Date_____

# of Holes	18	Par	70	Carts	YES	Clubs	YES

Yonkers

Sprain Lake Golf Course

290 E. Grassy Sprain Rd. • Zip 10710

Phone	(914) 779-5180
Hours Open	6:30 AM - dusk wkedays, 6 AM - dusk wkends
Average Green Fees	Res. $12/$15, Non. Res. $35/$40
Special Rates?	Senior Citizens, juniors
Credit Cards	No
Season	End of March - December
Amenities	Pro shop, putting green, restaurant, snack bar
Dress Code	Shirts must be worn at all times
Tee Time Required?	Call 285-GOLF for details
Golf Packages Available?	No
10% discount available?	Inquire

Validation_____Score_____Date_____

# of Holes	18	Par		Carts	YES	Clubs	YES

Yorktown Heights

Loch Ledge Golf Course

RR 118 • Zip 10598

Phone	(914) 962-8050
Hours Open	Daylight hours, semi-private, call for info
Average Green Fees	$15 - $20
Special Rates?	Senior Citizens M - F $7/9 holes w/cart
Credit Cards	MC/VISA
Season	Weather permitting - year round
Amenities	Pro shop, snack bar, deck overlooking 18th green, lessons
Dress Code	Proper golf attire
Tee Time Required?	Wkends
Golf Packages Available?	No
10% discount available?	Inquire

Validation_____Score_____Date_____

# of Holes	18	Par	71	Carts	$10	Clubs	$10

Yorktown Heights

Mohansic Golf Course

Baldwin Rd. • Zip 10598

Phone	(914) 962-4065
Hours Open	Daylight hours
Average Green Fees	$35 - $40
Special Rates?	Residents w/permit $12 - $15
Credit Cards	No
Season	April 1 - mid December
Amenities	Pro shop, lessons, bar, restaurant, driving range
Dress Code	No
Tee Time Required?	Phone reservations
Golf Packages Available?	
10% discount available?	Inquire

Validation_____Score_____Date_____

# of Holes	18	Par	70	Carts	$23	Clubs	YES

Arcade

Turkey Run Golf Course	11836 Bixby Hill Rd. • Zip 14009

Phone	(716) 492-2122
Hours Open	Daylight hours
Average Green Fees	$6 - $10 wkdays, $8 - $12 wkends & holidays
Special Rates?	No
Credit Cards	No
Season	April 1 - October 31
Amenities	With 2 tees
Dress Code	Shirts & shoes must be worn at all times
Tee Time Required?	No
Golf Packages Available?	No
10% discount available?	Inquire

Validation_____Score_____Date_____

# of Holes	9	Par	35	Carts	$8	Clubs	$2.50

Perry

Hidden Acres Par 3	Rt. 20A • Zip 14530

Phone	(716) 237-2190
Hours Open	Daylight hours
Average Green Fees	$6 wkdays, $6.50 wkends
Special Rates?	Season passes
Credit Cards	No
Season	Weather permitting - November 1
Amenities	Snack bar, putting green
Dress Code	Shirts must be worn at all times
Tee Time Required?	No
Golf Packages Available?	No
10% discount available?	No

Validation_____Score_____Date_____

# of Holes	9	Par	27	Carts	PULL	Clubs	YES

Pike

Rolling Acres Golf Course

7795 Dewitt Rd. • Zip 14130

Phone	(716) 567-8557
Hours Open	Daylight hours
Average Green Fees	$10 - $12
Special Rates?	Call for details
Credit Cards	MC
Season	May - October
Amenities	
Dress Code	No
Tee Time Required?	No
Golf Packages Available?	No
10% discount available?	Inquire

Validation_____Score_____Date_____

# of Holes	18	Par	70	Carts	$16	Clubs	$3

Varysburg

Byrncliff Resort & Conf

Humphrey Rd. & Route 20A • Zip 14167

Phone	(716) 535-7300
Hours Open	Daylight hours
Average Green Fees	$17 wkdays, $19 wkends
Special Rates?	No
Credit Cards	MC/VISA/AMEX/DISC/DINERS CLUB
Season	May - September
Amenities	Pro shop, bar, restaurant, putting greens, driving range for irons only, cross-country skiing, outdoor pool, tennis, lodging
Dress Code	Shirts must be worn at all times
Tee Time Required?	Yes
Golf Packages Available?	Call for details
10% discount available?	Inquire

Validation_____Score_____Date_____

# of Holes	18	Par	73	Carts	YES	Clubs	NO

Attica

Quiet Times Golf Course

Stedman Rd. • Zip 14011

Phone	(716) 591-1747
Hours Open	Daylight hours
Average Green Fees	$10
Special Rates?	Senior Citizens $9
Credit Cards	No
Season	May - October 31
Amenities	Snack bar
Dress Code	Shirts
Tee Time Required?	No
Golf Packages Available?	No
10% discount available?	Inquire

Validation_____Score_____Date_____

# of Holes	18	Par	62	Carts	$12	Clubs	$5

Fox Run Golf Course

4195 Route 14 • Zip 14878

Phone	(607) 535-4413
Hours Open	8 AM - dusk
Average Green Fees	$7.50
Special Rates?	No
Credit Cards	No
Season	May 1 - 1st snowfall
Amenities	Clubhouse
Dress Code	No
Tee Time Required?	No
Golf Packages Available?	No
10% discount available?	Inquire

Validation_____Score_____Date_____

# of Holes	9	Par	36	Carts	$8	Clubs	$3

INDEX

INDEX

This listing is by city first with the corresponding courses following in alphabetical order.